ACOB

YOU HAVE A DREAM

HOW TO FIGURE OUT WHAT THE HECK TO DO WITH YOUR LIFE

You Have A Dream: How To Figure Out What The Heck To Do With Your Life

By Jacob Hansen

Published by The Lionheart Press.
Springville, UT.
http://lionheartmentoring.com/

Cover by Kam Kaiserman - https://kamkaiserman.com/

ISBN: 978-1978030190

First Edition
First printing: October, 2017

This book is dedicated to:

The Lionheart Mentors,

My parents, Mike and Katie Hansen, and

All those who have blessed my life by believing in me.

TABLE OF CONTENTS

Dear Dreamer,

Do you ever find yourself wondering what the heck you want to do with your future?

Do you get the sense that it's time to take your life to the next level?

Do you want to make a big difference in the lives of other people?

If so, this book is for you.

Figuring out what you want to do with your life doesn't have to be characterized by feelings of discouragement, confusion, and straight up aggravation. If you know the principles behind dream discovery, it can be one of the most thrilling adventures of your life – just as adventurous as achieving and living it will be!

There are seven sequential steps that will lead any earnest seeker to a knowledge of the next mission they are called to live. I have broken down these steps throughout the following pages, and if you apply the associated strategies and principles into your life, I am confident that you will find the clarity that you need.

My story, as well as the stories of the youth and young adults told throughout this book, will show you the power that a dream has to shape your life for the better. We found hope, adventure, and purpose. So can you.

May the journey you take to your dream be filled with joy and victory.

Your friend,

Jacob Hansen

If the inquiries of others wasn't pressure enough for me to figure out what to do with my life, I had another, even greater awakening: this was *my life*, and I wanted to be successful! Though relatively young, I considered myself more than capable of taking action, learning, and doing incredible things – now that my ambition had woken up, I felt like a race car idling at an intersection, not sure which way to turn. I was ready to make something of myself, and that meant that I needed a direction to head in.

All of the sudden, my "I'll figure it out later" view of the future, failed me. And thus began my quest to figure out what the heck to do with my life.

Almost everyone will have to face this quest at least once in their lives, but there was one special trait that would turn my need to figure out my future, into a life-changing quest. This trait is also the reason I ended up in that rainy field. As I listened to other people talk about their lives, and as I looked at the opportunities around me, I saw a stereotypical path that looked something like this:

Graduate high school. Slave through college for another 4-6 years, maybe longer. Get a job that you kind of like. Look forward to weekends, holidays, and vacations. Work for 40 years. Retire, and go on more vacations. Eventually, die.

The prospect of living my life like that didn't jive with me. Like, not at all. I wanted my life to be awesome, and the stereotypical path wasn't going to cut it for me. That's when I began thinking about a mysterious phrase I had often heard people throw around:

"Follow your dreams."

What that phrase actually meant, I hadn't the foggiest idea. People say it, but they rarely tell you what a dream is, and almost never tell you how you're supposed to follow them. But despite not having any idea what that phrase was supposed to mean in practical application, I heard it promise something special – it hinted at a life that deviated from the stereotype in the best way possible. A dream sounded like something that would require my life to be passionate and fulfilling, maybe even adventurous.

At this point, I chose to take a big risk: as I set out to figure out where to take my life, I decided that I wasn't going to focus on what everyone else was doing, or what seemed "safe" and expected. Instead, I was going to become a dreamer! Because maybe, this whole idea of "Follow your dreams," would enable me to set my course for a truly incredible life.

If dreams truly existed, I was going to find one.

After three months of dedicated study, the help of mentors, and the deepest reflection of my life, this quest had lead me to a field in the middle of nowhere. I had armed myself with a list of critical questions, and was determined to answer them once and for all. My watch told me I had already been wandering for almost two hours. It was beautifully quiet. I was alone. The rain drizzled on.

I will find you. I mentally spoke to the elusive answers.

I climbed on a fallen log, and began to pace back and forward, racking my brain.

"What do I want in life?" I asked.

"Where should I go?"

"What should I do?"

At the core of them all, was the question "What is my dream?"

Two hours turned into three as I thought of greatest men and women in history: I wanted to be like them, but I also wanted to be me. I wanted greatness, I wanted to matter to the world, and I wanted to be a good man too. I wanted to love my life!

I thought about what I loved doing, about what I was good at, and about what big difference I wanted to make in the world. Rain trickled down my face, and I stared up at the afternoon clouds, light illuminating sporadic patches.

Wait a minute. I stopped pacing. *There's something...*

Like a ray of sunshine, an idea softly began to reveal in my mind. I suddenly became extremely excited – I hadn't discovered a road map, but I HAD found a vague destination! If I was right, I had caught the first glimpse of my dream!

I made a bold declaration that day. Before I was thirty years old, I would become two things: an internationally renowned speaker and writer, and an independently wealthy business owner. Why these two things? Because in the first case, I believe that truth has the power to change lives in every way, and I wanted to spread life-changing truth to as many people as possible. I also knew that if I was going to have maximum impact, I would need the freedom teach people without the financial and time constraints of a "normal" job. Not only that, but I've been a natural entrepreneur ever since my first lemonade stand, and I find it extremely fun. Hence, the business declaration.

Heedless of the rain, I launched myself off the log and jogged towards civilization. This new vision for my life was audacious and daring. It sounded like the most enjoyable challenge I had ever heard of! A fire burned in my soul, and I knew that my life would never be the same.

That evening, I eagerly met up with a mentor and small group of fellow students. We were meeting for a perfectly timed discussion about the projects we were going to work on over the next year. My peers had also been searching for a vision of where they wanted to take their lives, and the atmosphere was electric! We settled down around a dining room table for a discussion that would stretch late into the night. I remember feeling that anything was possible. My future was a clean slate, and now that I had an idea of what I wanted it to look like, I could get down to constructing my masterpiece. I scooted my chair in close and grabbed a pen.

"Where is my…" I had misplaced my notebook in my enthusiasm. *Dang it.*

Not to be deterred, I swiped a nearby napkin. It wasn't a Mona-Lisa level canvas for sure, but at a time of inspiration like this, I didn't care. To this day, that napkin remains one of my personal treasures.

As the meeting progressed, and as we shared our visions for the lives we wanted to live and the next steps we thought we should take, my thought process went something like this:

Okay Jacob, so you want to be a respected speaker and writer, correct?

Precisely.

Then you're going to have to have a great education and lots of credibility so people will want to listen to you.

Excellent point, brain. I guess I need to go to a good college. I wrote that down.

And you know that a classroom isn't going to give you all the speaking experience you need to get really good at influencing others.

Brilliant point! I'll seek out some real-world opportunities to hone my speaking skills. I wrote that down too.

Most entrepreneurs fail multiple times before hitting a homerun, so what if you started one right away and thereby get a ton of experience?

Where have you been all this time? Again I made a scribbled note on the napkin.

By the time we were done with our conversation, I had taken my bold declarations for the future, and created a plan to work towards entrance to the most difficult admission-level college in my state, master the art of oratory, and start my first business. This is me at fifteen, mind you. Don't worry, I thought I was crazy too.

Over the course of the next year, I would actually achieve all three of those goals! I was admitted to BYU two months after my sixteenth birthday, I won first place for my oratory skills at a speech and debate competition that pulled students from districts all over northern Utah, and I created Big Idea Children's Books, L.L.C. (That business didn't last long, but we did publish a book, sell and distribute it, and start production on a sequel).

When year two rolled around, I reevaluated my dream, found my next steps, and created a new plan. By the end of that year, I had been employed as a BYU faculty member and TA who got to sit down and coach first-year writing students on their papers. I had spent three weeks living in Japan on my own dime. A friend and I had created and grown a teen-to-teen idea hub, through which we published a few dozen self-help and inspirational articles and videos. Perhaps most importantly, this was in this year that I woke up to my dream on a significantly greater scale (more on this later).

As I write this book, I'm looking back over year three. This last year has been by far the best yet, in which I've dreamed up and led a movement among youth towards obliterating limitations and living a life of freedom, purpose, and service to others (known as the Lionheart movement). I've impacted thousands of people through this movement by becoming a nationally known youth speaker and mentor. I published my first book. I built my first *profitable* business, alongside the Lionheart movement, by camping out full time in my basement for six months with two of my best friends. I also became a national cabaret champion (a form of dance that combines ballroom with acrobatics), and ran two marathons.

I'm not telling you these things to brag about my list of accomplishments or pretend like my life is perfect. Honestly, there are a lot of people out there with similar and greater achievements, and I believe that your resume says very little about the quality of a person you are. My success has required me to face massive amounts of stress and discouragement, and I've made mistakes just like everyone else.

What I am showing you is that I have found my dream, and the pursuit of it has changed everything for me. Since the day I captured my first real glimpse of my dream, I've been living a whirlwind of opportunity, monumental challenges, victory, and straight-up-awesome-sauce! I am moving towards the fulfillment of my dream faster than I thought possible, and *every day it becomes more clear and compelling*. I absolutely LOVE my life, even through my most difficult, depressing, and disappointing days, for this reason: I know exactly where I need to be – that knowledge is among the sweetest life has to offer, and I would not trade it for the world.

As I write this, I am 18 years old. I'm a professional speaker, entrepreneur, mentor, student, dancer, and all around passionate dreamer. I'm a warrior, a champion for the heroes around me, and messenger of truth and light. I'm about to spend the next two years of my life off on a new adventure in Russia, teaching people, serving people, and taking my dream to a whole new level.

I've lived the last few years of my life in a radically different fashion than most people ever experience. The single greatest reason why, is this: I have a dream.

So too, you have a dream.

Are you, like I was, at a big decision point in your life? Do you need to find your next steps? Are you wondering what the heck you're supposed to do with your life?

Maybe you're not sure what path to take in high school. Maybe you're in your senior year, stressed out to the max because you don't know what college to attend. Maybe you're in college, dragging around an "undecided" major. Maybe you're about to jump into a career, but worry about the idea of staying there for a few decades. Maybe you're stuck without motivation because the things in your life aren't exciting to you. Maybe you're overwhelmingly busy, but you feel like in the midst of running around from commitment to commitment, you're missing something adventurous and meaningful.

If any of the above has struck a chord with you (or even described your life to a tee), then you're in the right place! I completely understand the pain of feeling at a loss for passionate direction in life. My good news for you, is that your future is completely yours to shape as you wish. The one thing that you're missing, is your dream.

And that's exactly what this book is here to help you discover.

I invite you to step away from the hamster wheel of asking where you should go to college, what you should major in, or what job you should get. Because if you don't know where you ultimately want to end up, it doesn't matter what path you take to get there. Before you get to any of those detailed questions, ask yourself what your dream is. The beauty of this shift of focus is that once you nail your dream, the rest of your answers will fall into place with relative ease.

Not only do you find direction for you life when you discover your dream, but it also sets you on *FIRE* (metaphorically speaking, of course)! Life becomes a grand and epic adventure when you're following your dream. Your work begins to really, really matter. Great challenges propel you towards unprecedented levels of learning and personal growth. You discover a thrill more sweet and enduring than any adrenaline-pumping sport. In the proper time, extraordinary achievement shows up as icing on the cake.

I've devoted a large portion of my life to coaching people on finding their dreams, virtually since the day I found mine. As I've studied and taught about this subject, I've come to understand three ideas that I believe, if lived, will change your life forever. I've written this book upon these three ideas, and as you read, you'll learn exactly how to live them. These ideas are worth taking note of:

1. You have a dream that is priceless to the world and powerfully unique to you.
2. You will find your greatest fulfillment, growth, and adventure in the pursuit of your dream.
3. You don't have to wait – you can begin to live your dream today.

My journey began because I knew that I had a dream. The result of my journey is knowing that you too have a dream. I've written this book to serve as a guide throughout the discovery of your dream, so that you can finally find your place and shape your destiny.

As you turn the pages of this book, you will learn from the stories of real youth and young adults who have discovered their dreams, as well as from a close look at the steps preceding the unveiling of my dream and it's early development. Along the way, I will lay out the seven step process through which *anyone* can find their own dream. These seven steps sequentially build upon one another, and are designed for you immediate application. Although the dreamers you will read about in this book are youth and young adults, the information presented to you is universal. It will help you whether you're nine or ninety years old.

If you read this book with an open mind and a passion to embark on the greatest adventure you've ever lived, then I promise that you will walk away with an understanding of the most important principles related to the study of your unique purpose in life. From there, it is your responsibility to act upon those principles. Ask yourself the big questions. Take inspired action. Seek out the people and information that you need. Commit to your future. Sacrifice to bless the lives of others. If you do this, you will inevitably be successful.

If you're ready to figure out what the heck to do with your life, today's your day.

Your dream, and the new life surrounding it, is right around the corner.

THE SEARCH FOR YOUR DREAM BEGINS

Do you remember how the discovery of my dream began? It didn't begin with my pacing around an epic rain-speckled field. That was a milestone moment, and definitely a defining tipping point. But I doubt that day would ever have come for me, had I not made a defining decision three months previous.

It was the day I decided that I wanted – *needed* – my dream, that it began to, ever so slowly, unveil before me. In the midst of pressure from others and great desire within myself, I committed to the path of searching for my dream. I chose to become a dreamer.

The first of the seven steps to discovering your dream and figuring out what that the heck to do with your life, is **Choose To Seek Your Dream**. Choosing to seek your dream means that you accept the idea that you have a dream, and then suit up to go find it. This requires you to think like a dreamer, talk like a dreamer, and act like a dreamer. Choosing to seek your dream requires a paradigm shift from reacting to what is "realistic" and expected, to requiring the extraordinary and audacious. It requires you to stop pouring your focus into getting a good job, and instead into identifying the purpose that your work in life will achieve.

When people ask what you're doing with your life, don't buy time by telling them about something that mildly peaks your interest. Instead, respond with something along the lines of "I'm in the middle of discovering my dream. I don't know exactly what it is yet, but I'm very excited!"

I guarantee that finding your dream possible. It might even be a lot easier to discover than you assume, especially if you take this first step to heart. So as you carry yourself through your day-to-day life, be confident in the chosen inevitability of your dream.

The core reason for this first step is simple: when you deliberately look for something, your chances of finding it drastically increase. You *might* stumble upon your dream in all it's glory by accident, but there are no guarantees. After all, the reason you're unsure of where to take your life is that your dream *hasn't* shown up on it's own. Looking for your dream is the first step.

This step should probably be obvious, but people often fail to understand the significance of it. If you skip this step, the benefit of knowing the next six steps is severely limited because you never consciously chose to begin the process in the first place.

Take a minute and imagine what your life would be like with if you had extreme clarity on where you wanted to go and what you wanted to achieve. Imagine how things would be different for you if you were on fire about life. Imagine how sweet it would taste to know that you were creating things that really mattered – to you and to others. Imagine how much you could grow if you were constantly pushed out of your comfort zone in the best way possible.

Now, take another minute and consider whether you're up to the task of working hard and pushing yourself to find the right answers. Consider whether you're ready to undertake the sometimes paralyzing fear of doing things that you've never done before. Consider whether you are willing to face rejection from people who don't understand you. Consider whether you're able to handle the stress of learning big lessons.

Pause your reading and secure a notebook, stack of papers, digital note taking system, or set of stone tablets for yourself. That is now your Dream Journal, and will be your companion from now on. In your newly formed Dream Journal, write out the greatest reasons that finding your dream matters to your life. Then, list out the biggest things that you are, and are not, willing to sacrifice in order to discover and live your dream. Don't cut corners or skip over this exercise. It will set a foundation for what lies ahead.

Now that you have a rough idea of what may be required of you, and the benefits you can reap from your dream, you need to ask yourself this critical question:

"Do I choose to dream?"

Dreams (and dreamers) get a lot of flack from the world, especially when they are young and just starting out. Living your dream is far from something that people talk about often, except in memes or jokes about eating fifty tacos while living in a mansion. Not only do most people rarely talk about their dreams or directly encourage you to find yours, but if you haven't already, you'll encounter people who fight against the whole idea of your dream.

Some people tell you that pursuing your dream is unwise or impractical. This is said by people who don't understand the power of a dream.

Some people declare that dreamers are naive and childish. These people have a misconceived idea of what a dream is.

Some people will flat out say that you can't live your dream because once you get out into the "real world," harsh reality will crush you. These are people who have allowed the difficulties of life to overpower them any dream that they once had.

In the eyes of the naysayers, any path that deviates from the status quo, the stereotype of "security," is risky. According to them, choosing to dream is risky. They might be right about that, but as the saying goes, "no risk, no reward." If dreaming is risky, that's a risk that I'll gladly take. Besides, doesn't living your life by blindly moving with the flow of easy opportunities and the pressures of others pose a far greater risk? By failing to take a risk on your dream, you could very easily end up doing everything "right," but never truly *living*.

So yes, I'm inviting you to take a risk, just as I did. Today is the day for you to commit to the search for your dream, no matter what opposition you may encounter. It's time for you to decide that if dreams exist, you're going to find one. Choose to take the risk of living life like you never have before.

In short, dare to dream.

The 7 Steps to Discovering Your Dream:

1. CHOOSE TO SEEK YOUR DREAM

If you want to find your dream, you need to deliberately search for it. Make the intentional choice to become a dreamer. Naysayers will call this process risky, but the greatest risk is never living at your highest potential. Decide that the answer to what YOU want to do with your life will be found by discovering your dream.

Two

THE BIG DREAM FORMULA

How do you turn the invisible into the visible? The first step is to define your dream precisely; the only limit to what you can achieve is the extent of your ability to define with precision that which you desire.
~ Tony Robbins

I'm about to blow your mind.

Or at least, I blew Andrea's mind, that's for sure.

It wasn't long after I started doing public speaking that I was invited to speak to a group of high schoolers and their parents at a conference about how to prepare for and plan for college. They wanted to me to talk about how I practically skipped high school and got admitted to the most competitive university in Utah by the age of 16. Which is a pretty cool accomplishment, I'll admit.

The truth was, however, that didn't happen just because I wanted to be an overachiever. The only reason I was able to be admitted under such abnormal circumstances was that I had a greater purpose backing me up – it wasn't about going to college for the sake of college, but instead, I had an idea of what my life was all about and that university was my next big step. So, that day at CollegeCon, I ditched my assigned topic and talked about this remarkable thing called a "Big Dream".

I walked into the conference breakout room and greeted a small group of about twenty people. I felt a bit nervous and inadequate to be running an event where I was going to tell my ambitious peers and their education-focused parents how they needed to change their mindset about higher education. I looked at the clock: barring severe embarrassment or boredom, these people were going to listen to me for the next forty-five minutes.

Whew. Alright then. I thought, *Here goes somethin'...*

I dove right in and started speaking. I shared my story, I taught a formula, I did some group exercises, and I asked some questions. I drove home a life-changing principle and shared with them what my dream looked like. It was awesome. When everyone had left, I gave a sigh of relief, packed up, and headed home.

Little did I know that something I had said wasn't going to be forgotten anytime soon. About a week later I got an email from the organizer of the conference. She forwarded me a message from one of the mothers who attended my workshop. She showed up with her teenage daughters, one of whom is Andrea. As I read her email, I couldn't stop smiling (slightly mischievously, I'm sure)!

She said that, in the words of her daughters, my class was «life changing." For Andrea, it completely flipped her plans upside down: «One of my girls thought she wanted to be a nurse until a simple exercise he had us do in class,» this mother wrote. «Now she knows she wants to pursue architectural design.»

Hold up, hold up. From nurse to architect based off of one simple exercise? Mind = blown.

And Andrea isn't the only one these principles have worked for, either. When CollegeCon invited me to speak the following year, I packed my room at standing-room-only, three different times, full of people who wanted to find their dream and figure out what the heck to do with their lives!

Now, this is the point where I give you a fair warning. If you already have some underwhelming, responsible, or even ambitious plans for you future that you really don't want tampered with, you should probably stop reading here. Trust me, it will save you an internal dilemma, because the simple principles, formulas, and exercises I'm going to share with you in the next few pages (and throughout the whole book) have the potential to seriously alter the course of your life. So if you already have plans up to this point, be prepared to create *even better* ones!

But that's the reason you're reading this book. You know life has more to offer you than you have at this moment, and you want an incredible epiphany that will set you on a course for the most wild adventure you've ever lived!

As I've lived my dream and taught others to live their own dreams, it has been my joy and privilege to see many youth and young adults, just like you and I, discover their dream. You'll find that it's one of the most thrilling experiences to see a person's eyes light up at a glimpse of their next mission. Especially if that person is you! So get ready for cutting edge information about what a dream is. For some of you, this will blow your mind. For others it will seem completely obvious because deep down you've had a sense of it all along.

Have you ever walked into a room to get something, and immediately forgot what you were looking for? Yeah, me too! In that situation, it's almost impossible to retrieve the desired object until you return to whatever it was you were doing beforehand and slap yourself in the face when you remember what you needed.

Knowing what you're looking for makes finding it a LOT easier to find. Accordingly, the second step to discovering your dream and figuring out what the heck to do with your life, is **Know What You're Looking For**.

You might think of this as a step so obvious that it's not worth writing about, but look at it this way: your Instagram feed is probably is covered with inspirational pictures of athletes and landscapes featuring phrases such as "Follow your dream," "Live your dream," "Remember your dream," "Never give up on your dream," and "Dream big." Maybe you even have a Pinterest board dedicated to these quotes (who am I to judge?). But if you were given ten seconds or less to explain to me what a 'dream' was, could you?

I certainly couldn't when I first started out. I probably would have said that a dream was, "Something that people aspire to and want to achieve." Is that true of a dream? Sure it is! But SO MUCH is missing if that's all of a definition you have to work with, because if that's what you want, that's what you'll get.

I, for one, aspire to not being sleep deprived and want to achieve a nap this weekend. Depending on how tired I am, such a goal could be very motivating, but I just don't feel the epic grandeur of a new life adventure coming from it. Get my vibe?

Our culture is in the middle of an epidemic of people wishing they could have something (or telling people not to pursue something) that they don't understand. The problem is simply that the world doesn't have a good definition for the powerful force called a dream or an understanding of it's inner workings in the lives of people – dreams move the human spirit like gravity moves matter. But if you look it up 'dream' in the dictionary, most of the definitions you'll read describe what happens when you're sleeping! Thank you, napping aspiration.

Having a better understanding of what the dream that you're looking for consists of is important for everyone, no matter where you currently are in the process of discovering your dream. Some people just *know* intuitively what their dream is – or at least part of it – and most other people wonder why they didn't get delt those lucky cards because they haven't the slightest idea what they want to be when they grow up. No matter which group you're in, the more clarity you possess, the easier it will be to find (and achieve) what you really, truly want.

Do you remember in the first chapter when I told you the story about how my journey of dream discovery began one day when I made the conscious choice to seek out my dream? That choice happened months before I experienced my epic moment of wilderness inspiration. The journey began when I first began to realize that I had a lot of big decision to make in life, and that if I wanted to be *phenomenal*, it would be useful for me to get a head start on my dream, especially as a young teenager.

My ultimate problem was, I had no idea what I wanted to do with my life! The bane of any inspired person is a lack of direction; if you have ever been without a lack of personal vision or focus for any extended amount of time, you know exactly what I mean.

So naturally, I did what anyone in my situation must inevitably do: I got fired up and set out to find my dream. Day one of my quest to figure out what the heck to do with my life (aka Operation: Big Dream), was suddenly in full swing.

Back then, my understanding of a dream was mostly limited to your Instagram feed "live your dream" cliches. Fortunately for me, however, I had something special on my side: I didn't have to figure out how to live an awesome life all on my own. Specifically, I had a few incredible friends and mentors who pointed me in the right direction when I asked them about dreams.

On the second day of my quest I showed up at school to begin a new semester-long group. I mean, we technically called ourselves a class, but it definitely wasn't your traditional class – we had six students and two teachers. The purpose of the class was to assist us students in preparing for future education and life by building projects in the real world, based on what we were passionate about or subjects we felt we needed to work on. Sounds pretty perfect for where I was at in my dream journey, right?

I can still remember walking confidently into our small classroom for the first time on a January afternoon. The afternoon sun was shining through the single window. I set my backpack on the ground and pulled up a chair next to my best friend at the folding table we were all gathered around. I had a close relationship with every student and mentor at that table, and I was excited to get started. With what, I wasn't exactly sure. But I got the sense that if there was anywhere I could discover what a dream was, it would be here.

Though I didn't realize it at the time, I had just stepped onto the dream team. In a matter of weeks we would all be engaged in radically different pursuits (composing music, reading up on psychology, studying for college entrance exams, getting less sleep than is healthy, etc.), but through the difficulty of getting started we would be there to hold each other accountable and use our cheerleading skills to support one another when the going got rough. I wasn't the only one born for greatness, and I didn't have to walk this journey alone.

You don't either. Even though some people play the role of "naysayers" in our lives, there are also many people who want to see you succeed in discovering your dream. These champion figures will support, encourage, or guide you as soon as you reach out. So don't worry; you don't have to do it all on your own! Doing it all on your own is, in fact, an unnecessarily tedious and time-consuming process.

Some people, when searching for their life purpose, feel the need to take their time. They move from one thing to another, patiently waiting for inspiration to strike them like Paul on the road to Damascus. They move with the flow of life until they have personally collected all the direction and opportunity they think they need to be successful.

I am NOT one of those people.

Through my years of living and studying dreams, I have learned that although you need an unmeasurable amount of time for your dreams to grow and develop inside you before they are mature enough for exponential success, *you always have enough information and resources to take action on your dream right now*. Even if you don't think you know what you want out of life, you can still move towards your dream. If you're feeling stuck because you don't know what you want, that doesn't have to hold you back from taking steps right now to discover your dream. Besides, you can't know how long it will take you to prepare for success. It might take you years, and you might be ready this very moment. You may as well start now!

On day three of Operation Big Dream, I still didn't know what I wanted or what my big dream would look like when I found it, so on that day I began to study the ideas of successful people who already knew how to live awesome lives, and were in the business of teaching other people how to do so. This was my greatest shortcut to the discovery of my dream. On the one hand, I could sit in a cave for five years and philosophize about the "good life", or on the other hand, I could read a book in five hours, discuss the book with my parents and mentors, and then go practice living the good life. One of those options appealed to me a lot more than the other, and I'll let you guess which. (No offence, Descartes.)

To the end of discovering what a big dream was through study, I committed myself with focus and passion comparable to that which my dog has while chasing a car down the street. If you're one of the more patient people out there who feel content waiting for your dream to knock at your door, I totally respect that. It's your life, after all, and you can live it however you want.

Personally, I prefer a faster and more direct path, because I feel a great sense of urgency about my time here on earth – I want to *do* the most meaningful things possible, and if a dream is a necessary piece of knowledge, I want to find it as fast as possible. I therefore chose to seek out and learn from as many mentors and like-minded peers as I could find. I collected audio recordings, YouTube videos, articles, worksheets, and the advice of real people.

On week two of Operation Big Dream, I started reading books. A LOT of them. Some books I read multiple times, such as *The Element* and *Finding Your Element* by Sir Ken Robinson, and *The Dream Giver* by Bruce Wilkinson. While digesting these books I would think about my dream almost non-stop. I took copious notes on my lessons I learned, and began to put together sections of my puzzle piece by piece. As the weeks went by I compiled a list of questions designed to provoke the answers I needed. These were questions such as:

"What are my highest priorities?"

"What is my ELEMENT?"

"Am I willing to pay the ultimate price?"

And over two dozen other pivotal questions, which I have since used to teach dreamers how to take their dream to the next level.

By the time month three of Operation Big Dream drew to a close, I was ready. I had completed the second step on the road to discovering my dream – I knew what I was looking for, and now it was time to get some serious answers.

A few days later, I was running home through a rain-misted countryside, on fire about the beginnings of the dream I had just discovered within myself. Though that day was pivotal, it came only after I learned what I was looking for.

To take the second step towards finding your dream, you must likewise know what you're looking for. You must decide for yourself what the perfect dream will look like for you when you find it; how it's going to affect you and others. You've got to do this for *yourself* because if it's not *your* dream, it doesn't matter if you find it.

That said, I can save you a lot of time through this book (about three years of study and application, if my experience is any indicator). You might have to go on a study rampage like I did for three months, but if you pay close attention to what I'm about to share with you, you'll probably be able to take this step in an hour or two.

I have found that while you need to decide for yourself what a dream means to you, the *type of dream that pushes people to their best selves, unlocks new* adventures, and enables them to do something that really, truly matters in a big way in this world, is going to be one that ultimately fits this definition:

> ## *Dream*
>
> **Your dream is a personalized mission** to create or accomplish a specific outcome directed by a desire to serve others, fuelled by your passions, and made possible by your natural aptitudes. It encompases a deliberate phase of time in your life, its fulfilment requires you to become something greater than you now are, and it is a mission you and you alone are perfectly prepared for.

That definition of a dream is worth the weight of this book in gold. If I ever find this copy and notice that you haven't highlighted or otherwise marked it down, we're going to have to have a serious talk. Yeah, I'm talking to you. Just do it.

Now let's get some common misconceptions out of the way and talk about what a dream is NOT:

A dream is NOT a lifestyle. This is by far the most common misinterpretation of a dream. When people think about their "dream," their first mistake is often to conjure up images of owning a mansion, traveling the world, having perfect abs, driving a lamborghini, posting to a million instagram followers, and sleeping in until whatever they want. Those can be *awesome* lifestyle goals to strive for, but alone, they aren't a dream and they won't lead you to greatness, impact on the world, or even day to day fulfilment and happiness. The world is full of people who live the "dream lifestyle" who are also unhappy, unfulfilled, and who can't escape the feeling that they're missing something big in their lives. The truth is, a dream is not defined by the place you live, the car you drive, the money you make, or the fame you collect.

A dream is so much more than what the world commonly praises as "success." You may find wild amounts of that type of success along the path to your dream, and you might not. It won't matter though, because the dream is what you actually want. A dream is purpose that you know deep in your heart that you were created to bring about. It's a personal mission to do or become something unique and powerful. It's a vision of possibility that sets you on fire about life; something that you can lie in bed late into the night planning for, and then jump out of bed early in the morning to take action on. It's a direction and a set of goals that push you to the very limit, but for which you will gladly sacrifice everything but your personal values to achieve. It's a distant result that breathes life into your soul even when you're required to fail for years before achieving it.

If you win the world's version success at the expense of your dream, you'll find the greatest loss of all. Win your dream first, and the other success you want will fall into its proper place in your life.

A dream is NOT a person. I don't care how long you've been together or how much you love her, but the girl of your dreams is not your dream. I've seen far too many social media users who seem to think otherwise. The people in your life will play a critical role in helping you live your dream, and they may even be part of the fulfilment of your dream. But under no circumstances is the affection of another person a proper substitute for your dream. Ew...no. Don't even go there.

A dream is NOT something your brain does when you're sleeping. Because if so, my dream is to show up without pants to my own wedding and/or fight Darth Vader with my aggravatingly slow motion kickboxing skills. Just, no. Of course, this isn't to say that you can't dream up your dream or have nocturnal dreams about its achievement, it's just...well, I think you know the difference.

A dream is NOT a career. Limiting your dream to a career is essentially just a way of living the stereotype we rejected in the first chapter, but in a way where it's not horrible. Definitely an improvement, but not a dream. The dreams you live should shape your career, not the other way around.

A dream is NOT a goal. A goal is like a milestone. Your dream is the destination. If your dream becomes merely the tactics through which you could accomplish a great mission, then you run the risk of traveling forever without ending up anywhere you really want to be.

A dream is NOT a life purpose. Although your dream and your purpose are closely connected, they are not the same thing. Many people find their purpose and stop there; a rookie mistake, easily corrected. Your purpose is about who you are and what you're all about in life. A dream is what you get to do next to fulfil on that purpose.

At Lionheart Mentoring (the organization behind the Lionheart movement), we've been discussing the difference between a purpose and a dream since day one. Quiana, fellow mentor and co-founder of the movement, has a beautiful and very simple purpose: "To uplift, enlighten and inspire." I learned about Quiana's purpose within the first few days of meeting her. She wore her purpose like a magnificent badge, and was quick to talk about it.

That purpose isn't her dream though. She has a long-term dream of becoming a world-renowned author and impacting the world through telling stories. Along the way, her purpose has taken the immediate and individual form of dreams such as creating Lionheart Mentoring. Her purpose is critical, and it's part of who she is. It will be woven through everything she does. It is also not her dream.

If you listen to enough people tell you their purpose, you'll notice a pattern emerge. Although the words change from person to person, the most authentic and positive purposes are connected by this universal theme:

To have joy and to give joy to others.

Included on the road to joy are elements such as freedom, love, power, prosperity, truth, exploration, protection, education, creation, and so forth. We each approach the purpose of joy from different angles, but the best and brightest purposes will ultimately seek it in some form.

A dream differs from this unified life purpose. A dream is where individuality and timing come into play, so that you can know what adventurous mission you are specifically called to in this phase of your life.

Have you ever thought that your dream was one of those things? If you have, know that you're in good company! I've done that before, and so has just about everyone. The important part is that you started dreaming in the first place – props to you!

Now the next step is to get excited because as good as what you thought your dream was, the next level of your dream will be even better. In contrast to what a dream is not, here is a list of some of the main things that a dream IS:

A dream IS scary. Your dream will force you to confront your greatest fears and insecurities because you must rise above them in order to achieve it. Oftentimes we unconsciously blind ourselves to major pieces of our dreams because we're scared of failing at them. If you find fear, don't run from it. Not all fear is useful, but it could very well be that your fear is a very obvious signpost on the road to your dream.

A dream IS powerful. A dream is one of the greatest long-term motivators known to mankind. It will pull you through thick and thin, and give you the desire to push through every obstacle imaginable. It is a creed written upon your heart that you will stop at nothing to achieve. It's something you will sacrifice your sleep, food, and comfort for (within reason) and still be completely on fire about.

A dream IS educational. The fastest way to learn life lessons is to stick your neck out into the world when the stakes are high. The fastest way to internalize facts and information is to seek our such knowledge when you are highly driven to apply it. Your dream combines both of those elements into what I call need-based learning, which is the most effective way to learn known to human beings. Because of what it will require of you and lead you to do, your dream can be thought of as a personalized curriculum for the next phase of your life.

A dream IS BIG. In your life you've probably found and lived little dreams, like meeting a favorite singer, winning a competition, or landing the perfect college job. These are analogous to your dream, in that they thrill you and leave you feeling successful and happy afterwards. And in fact, such dreams are often milestones along the road to the achievement of your Big Dream. Your dream is like a little dream, just, well...bigger! In this context, big doesn't mean that your dream has to involve millions of people or be something popular or make you a ton of money or anything like that. Finding a dream that's big means that you don't settle for playing small in your life, and you push yourself to ambitiously test your personal limits. As you learn more and more about your dream, you will see it grow and expand to a point where it's so big that you might even doubt your capacity to handle it – you can, but it's going to take everything you've got.

A dream IS for others. Think for a moment and imagine that you are at the end of your days, on your deathbed looking back over your life. Now ask yourself this: of everything I've done, what matters most to me? (Now would be a great time to record your answer in your Dream Journal.)

At the end of our lives, most of us will look back over our years on earth and take a personal inventory. When I think about what really matters to me, I realize that, at the end of my life, it won't matter how much money I make, how many trophies I have on my shelf, or how many followers I have on social media. What will really matter is whether or not I loved the people around me.

Is there a better way to love someone than to serve them? I believe that one of the greatest parts of a dream is its focus on blessing the lives of others. Love is our greatest motivator, and service our greatest fulfilment. Your dream in its most pure form is designed to serve and bless those around you.

Coryne, an 18-year-old girl whose dream includes becoming an aerospace engineer, put it perfectly when she wrote to me about how discovering her dream has impacted her life: "I've...become so much more service oriented. I've found that life gives you so much that the only way to hold it all is by giving some of it back."

Your dream IS YOU. Your dream is the perfect expression of who you are. That's why it's so powerful. That's why it's so needed. You feel a deep inner pain when your dream is missing, because part of *you* is missing – the most brilliant, happy, and impactful version of you will only be born through the living of your dream. (More on this in the next chapter.)

THE BIG DREAM FORMULA

Now that you have a good idea of what a dream is and is not, it's time for your knowledge of what you are looking for in the quest for your dream to become extremely practical. Are you ready for the "simple exercise" that blew Andrea's mind? After the months I spent studying for my dream paid off, the inspiration for a formula I call the Big Dream Formula fell into my life. This formula could very well be the last piece of information you need for your vision to finally start clicking together. I know that certainly has been the case for many dreamers.

One such dreamer is young woman named Kess. I've had the privilege to watch her embark on the same journey you are now on – to discover her extraordinary dream. She's on the fast track to the fulfilment of her dream, and I'm incredibly proud of her.

"I've been in love with dance my whole life," Kess writes, "But in 2016 I decided I wanted to be a dance teacher when I grew up. All it was at that point was an idea, but I loved it!" Kess had been dancing for years, in styles from ballet to ballroom.

"Then I started going to some Lionheart Mentoring events," she continues, "and I was like 'Wow, they're talking about big dreams. I want to find my big dream!' And as I went to the events and learned the big dream formula, my big dream developed. I found out that my love of dance and my talent for dance could change the world. And I didn't have to wait till I was older! My big dream is to help people express their emotions in healthy ways like through dance, art, and music. And I never would have found that without the big dream formula. I am currently working towards and actively pursuing my big dream, and it's AWESOME! It might be a long journey, and sometimes I get discouraged. But I am choosing to rise above, and dare to dream."

Kess is a powerful dreamer, and if you look closely, you'll be able to see each element of the Big Dream Formula applied in her story. This formula is powerful because it applies the second step towards finding your dream by teaching you about what your dream is and how powerful it can be, and also by guiding your focus as you seek for further clarity. The inputs to the formula are truths that you can easily recognize, and the outcomes are *clues* as to what your dream will be – it can give you incredible insight, and those insights will be the perfect place for you to piece together your dream.

Are you ready to swan dive into the fountain of dream knowledge? Let's break down the Big Dream Formula. For this exercise, you'll need your Dream Journal, so pull it out and draw three circles that overlap such that you create a Venn diagram.

(A note to serious readers: if your Dream Journal is still empty – or you haven't put one together yet – you should stop reading right here and go do that. All done? We good now.)

In my experience living my own dreams and teaching hundreds of others about how to live theirs, I have found that every worthwhile dream is a personal combination of three critical elements:

1. Passion - Once upon a time, Jacob Hansen looked around at the world and decided that no dream would be good enough for him unless it could stroke a fire of joy within him as he took the daily steps towards living it. Your dream can do the same for you! You'll definitely have your ups and downs along your road to living it, but for the most part, your dream will be filled with activities that you genuinely enjoy doing and that you can get into the zone about and forget about how fast the clock moves. Write My Passion in the first circle. This is part one of the formula. On your page, make a long list of the things that you love doing the most in life.

Just to be clear, we're not talking about eating a pound of dark chocolate while binge watching a season of Psych. You may enjoy that too, but what you need to focus on for this formula to work are the things that you could do for hours on end because they make you come ALIVE. The advice to "follow your heart" is so popular in our world today because most often, passion is what's missing in people's lives. Is it missing in yours? Pay close attention to the things that you love to DO, not just the things you like to experience – add all these things to your list.

What do you love doing so much that you lose all track of time?

2. Aptitude - When optimistic people tell you to do what you love, a group of "realists" always seems to pop up somewhere who tell you the "do what you love" stuff is bad advice and that dreamers like you are irresponsible. To a certain degree, these naysayers just need to take a chill pill, because living a dream will, from time to time, require you to do something thing that other people think is crazy, stupid, and devoid of all reason. But our less-than-optimistic friends actually do have a point: they notice that your passions aren't the only thing you should be considering when you're setting out to figure out what the heck to do with your life.

The truth is, your aptitudes are as much a part of your dream as your passions. You are a unique individual with a mix of skills, abilities, talents, and experience that no one else on the planet has. These natural aptitudes – both the gifts and the limitations – are a core part of who you are. Do you really think that the missions you're called to achieve in this world will overlook them? That would be like telling a fish that his dream wouldn't be found anywhere in the water.

In the next circle in your Venn diagram, write My Aptitudes and make a list of them. This is the second part of the formula.

An aptitude may be something that you're currently a master at, but it doesn't have to be. Some people have spent their whole lives practicing skills that aren't in alignment with their true aptitudes. One of the best ways to know what your aptitudes are is to listen to the people around you. Look for times when people say things like "Wow, you're brilliant at this...did you miss your calling in life?" Or when they say "How did you do that?" and you shrug and admit that you just kind of figured it out by accident. Another way to identify your aptitudes is to pay attention to what subjects and skills you understand and pick up easily.

So answer this question: *What do you find comes easily to you, or what do people say you have a natural gift for?*

3. Need - I use the word "need" here not to refer to your personal needs, but to the needs of other people. The problems in the world that stir your soul. The opportunities you have to bless the lives of others in big, meaningful ways.

Ask the average high school or college student what they want to do with their life, and studies show that they probably won't know for sure. But what they will say, is that they want to do something that makes an *impact* on the world. Do you want the same thing? Of course you do! I believe this is because a core part of our nature as human beings is connected with a desire to do something big to help other people. What's more, it is through our service to others that we achieve true greatness. As actor Jim Carrey put it in a speech to a graduating high school class about finding your dream, "The effect you have on others is the most valuable currency there is."

Ultimately, your dream is not about you. If you make it about you, you'll get stuck. A dream's most important power and value comes from the service that you do for others through the living of it. Just think about how your motivation and speed of action changes when you're making sacrifices for someone that you care about versus for your own benefit.

Write Needs of Others in the last circle. This is the third and final input to the formula. Make a list of the problems in the world that you think should be solved the most, and the needs that you feel strongly about providing for.

What problems are there in the world and what needs do other people have that you care most deeply about?

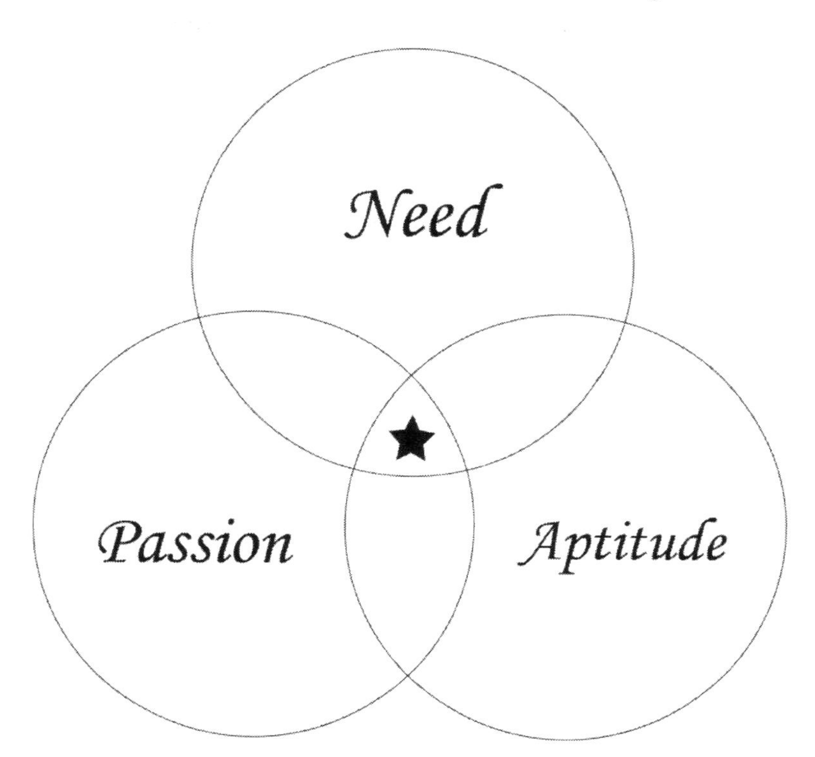

You have now completed the formula! You have three lists, and your next task is to see where all three intersect. Where your passions, aptitudes, and the needs of others combine into one, is where you find clues as to what your dream is. Boom. There you have it!

Passion + Aptitude + Need = Dream (the starting point of it)

Take a good look at that completed formula. Then, burn it into your memory. This is the exact formula for knowing what you're looking for. This is not just a dose of well-intentioned advice given over a warm hug and a plate of cookies. This is the real deal.

Obviously, the center of your Venn diagram represents where you find clues about your dream. But if you look into the blank spaces where only two circles intersect, you can learn how powerful the backstage benefits of a dream are.

When you combine your greatest passions and aptitudes, you find yourself in a position where you love doing something that you're also naturally good at. This means you have everything it takes to put in the long, dedicated hours required to achieve mastery at something, and if necessary, become the world's best at the actions of your dream.

When you combine your passions with the needs of others, you find fulfilment. No matter how numerically successful you become, when you're serving others in the way you love best, you'll find a sweet feeling of fulfilment that no amount of money can ever buy.

Speaking of money, what happens when you combine the needs of others with your mature aptitudes? The laws of business say that if you're really good at solving other people's problems, you have the potential to make a lot of money.

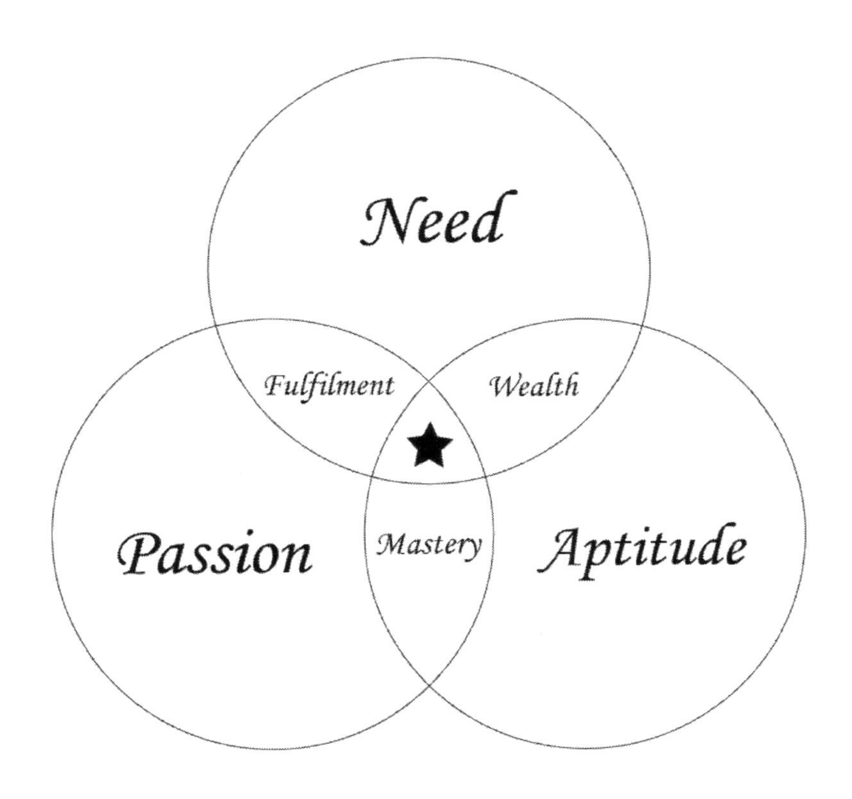

Some people include money itself into their Big Dream Formula, saying that you need to look for a dream that is economically practical. That isn't necessary, however, because if you're truly living your dream, you'll always find a way to make it work in the long run. In fact, if you want to make a lot of money, the best option is to look for your dream, not the money. If you look at the money your thinking will be limited to what other people have already created.

Take Henry Ford for example: he didn't take a high paying job in a company that built carriages. He followed a dream instead, and revolutionized the world! And you can bet that he made bank doing so. If you're filling a real need in the world, then no matter what your dream is, there's more than enough money for you to be successful at it. So don't worry about the money. If you worry about the money, you'll handicap the search for your dream and possibly spend a large portion of your life running after money only to realize in the end that it cost you your dream. Focus instead on what you actually want out of life. Because in your complete dream, you'll be providing the most value to others that you can, and the world has a way of reimbursing that value handsomely.

HOW TO KNOW WHAT YOU'RE LOOKING FOR

At the beginning of this book, I told you the story of how I discovered my big dream for the first time. As I wandered over fences and fields that spring day, I asked myself many questions; every question was derived from the Big Dream Formula and the truths about what a dream is and what it is not. Before that turning point occurred in my life, I had already taken the second step towards finding your dream. I knew what I was looking for.

After I figured that out, my searching revealed a future as an internationally renowned speaker and author, and an independently wealthy entrepreneur. The revelation showed up feeling like a ray of sunshine, and I thought to myself, "Of course! That's so perfect!" I felt a joy of inspiration, and a fire was lit within my soul.

If you take the time to know what you're looking for, you too can find your dream.

Your assignment is to use your Dream Journal in collaboration with this chapter to write out or mark your own picture of the requirements you have for your dream. What will your dream look like? What will it feel like? How will you know when you've found it? How big do you want it to be?

This second step to figuring out what the heck you want to do with your life can take some serious time and work (it took me three months, and while I didn't have this book to help me along, it will still take effort from you). But if you think about it, is there a more important homework assignment that setting the course for the rest of your life?

Go apply the Big Dream Formula and complete the above assignment. Get quiet, and get serious. Do the work, and don't skimp. It's time for you, finally, to decide what you want from this magnificent life.

No study is more worth your time. Because if you don't know what you're looking for, how on earth do you expect to find it?

The 7 Steps to Discovering Your Dream:

1. CHOOSE TO SEEK YOUR DREAM

If you want to find your dream, you need to deliberately search for it. Make the intentional choice to become a dreamer. Naysayers will call this process risky, but the greatest risk is never living at your highest potential. Decide that the answer to what YOU want to do with your life will be found by discovering your dream.

2. KNOW WHAT YOU'RE LOOKING FOR

The more clearly you can define what you want, the more direct your path to obtaining it will be. Study the principles and formulas that characterize dreams. Write out your life purpose. Reflect on your passions, aptitudes, and the needs of the world. Take the time to decide how you'll know YOUR dream when you find it.

Three

YOU ARE A HERO

You have a choice; choose to be free.
~ Lionheart slogan

It was the spring of 2015, and in the midst of a Utah world blooming with sunshine, flowers, and green trees, I was spending most of my time camping out in my dark basement, working on my computer. I was in the middle of dreaming up a new project with one of my friends, and it didn't leave much time for trivial things like Vitamin D. I was like an inspired monk – or Gollum, depending on how you look at it.

Much had happened in the months after I made my dream-defining resolutions amongst mentors and fellow students. It had been almost a year since my day of wilderness meditation. My carefully laid plan was paying off, and now, at sixteen years old, I was making relatively quick progress towards my vision for what I wanted to be in life. I had been accepted to my prefered college, started (and failed!) a business, and collected some medals for my public speaking skills – everything was proceeding as I had foreseen.

What I did not foresee was the specific reason I was sitting in a basement without natural lighting: I had become a blogger! (At this point I've decided to wholeheartedly embrace the fact that I was, and probably still am, a nerd. It least this nerd has good personal hygiene.)

For a handful of previous semesters, a friend and classmate of mine, Celine, had worked together on many of our papers and school writing assignments. Over the recent school year we had started publishing our best pieces on a blog together, in hopes of inspiring people to think about great ideas. We had published casually for many months, but this spring we both began to feel that we needed to do something bigger. That feeling lead to a pivotal conversation over video call one afternoon that went something like this:

"Most teenagers," Celine said, her voice a bit muffled due to the mediocre wifi connection, "Need a good ol' slap upside the head to remind them that they don't have to be apathetic do-nothings." We were talking about the deplorable situation social media had painted for us about the average teenager.

"It's true," I replied. "Because the truth is, teenagers are *totally* capable of doing *amazing* things. But most of them never try because they don't believe that they can; society just expects them to be irresponsible and not to care about anything but having fun, partying, and doing stupid things."

"And just because you're young doesn't mean that you can't go out there and actually change the world," Celine pointed out. "Or at the very least, get a head start on your life instead of wasting your time! Like, there is SO much you can be doing with reading books alone." She was an avid reader and we had discussed many a worthwhile book (plus a few others that were the time investment equivalent of watching Transformers. Aka, lamesauce).

"And if you think about it, when you're young is actually the perfect time to try to do great things," I continued. "Because even if you fail, you don't have a lot of responsibility – like providing for a family or whatever – and you have a lot of years ahead of you, so you can keep learning and trying again with basically no risk!"

We were getting pretty fired up by this point.

After throwing around examples of the low expectations our peers were too frequently immersed in, and countering with stories of incredible youth who did incredible things with their pre-20's years, we sparked a big, life-changing idea:

We would use our blog to build a teen-to-teen think tank with the purpose of creating a culture of excellence in the lives of youth. Wala! We were about to start using our shared aptitudes and passions to attempt to fill a fundamental societal need. The world had better be ready, because this was our time to shine!

"If we're going to do this," Celine noted with great gravity and growing excitement, "We've got to go BIG. Like not just our friends, but like, we need to at least take this to the national level. If we're actually going to change the culture of teenagers, this needs to be HUGE."

"Totally!" I exclaimed passionately. At this point, my excitement was so great that I could barely refrain from running in circles and climbing on things. "Dude, can you IMAGINE what the world would be like if it was cool to treat other people with respect and work hard and read books and talk about things that really mattered?!? We need to create a culture where youth are expected to be great and do great things, and where they actually strive to be their best!"

With that, the two of us set out to change the world. I have and will continue to set out on many such epic journeys throughout my life, but this monumental day was the first moment in which I confronted an audacious quest that was perfectly cut out for me, and accepted the call with complete determination. I didn't know how, but I knew *why*, and that was enough for me.

Don't you love how, when confronted with a problem we felt deeply about, our natural response was to say "Alright then, let's go change the world! Not just our friend group, but through the internet, all the teenagers in America?"

With the benefit of hindsight, I realize we were not far off from what some people would diagnose as crazy. That said, you might have said the exact same thing. Prudence and patience are useful attributes, but you'll naturally learn them as you gain experience and practice at the whole "living" thing. Your natural ambition and perspective of possibility, on the other hand, is one of the core reasons why it's the perfect time for you to find your dream and get moving towards it. One of the most powerful attributes of being young is that it's easy to be audacious because you naturally don't see many things as impossible. Except maybe getting a date for Friday...but that's a conversation for a different book.

As we sat planning on that video call, Celine and I stood on the edge of creating something that we felt truly mattered; we were facing a mission to remind our peers of their powerful potential! I believe I speak for both of us when I say that I felt on fire! I felt alive, and I felt AWESOME. I felt unstoppable. In a word, I felt like a hero. A freakin' *hero.*

Have you ever lived a moment in which you felt, as I did, like a hero? Perhaps it was at the start of a new adventure, or at the end of a great achievement. Maybe you just woke up early one morning and felt ready to take on the world.

I've certainly had my ups and downs, but through thick and thin I've always held with me a belief that I was destined for something great in life. Starting as young as I can remember, I would look to the future and think to myself, "Of course I'll do something fantastic and glorious and important when I grow up!" I knew I had great potential, and I knew that I wasn't interested in living an "average" or "normal" life. To me, greatness was a real, even expected, possibility for my future. I believed that I was strong, capable, and that, just like the heroes I admired, I could someday change the world.

As a child, it never worried me that I didn't know what I wanted to do with my life, because I somehow knew that whatever it was, it would be worthy of a great story. When I was six years old, for example, I was debating the most exciting professions I could think of: an astronaut, soldier, or local bus driver. I had weighed the pros and cons, but my child self couldn't quite make up my mind as to which of those three was best.

Despite this, I believed my mother with all my heart when she said that I could do anything I put my mind to. And for me, that would mean extraordinary impact and success. My childhood was not perfect (no one's ever is), but never once did I have cause to doubt that I – put simply – was a hero.

Did you once feel that way as well?

Was there a moment in your existence when you believed that life would ultimately go your way, that you would get a happily-ever-after, and that you would have the opportunity to face and overcome intimidating obstacles?

Have you ever wanted to be a hero?

Heck yes! Of course you have! It's part of our nature as human beings to want to do and be something meaningful. No matter how deeply hidden, there is a spark of hope within you that knows that you are destined for something more than what life has given you.

You might have forgotten this divine part of you, but I believe that if you're willing to seriously reflect on your deepest desires, you'll remember it. If you're still reading this book, it's likely that you know deep within you that you were born for great things in this life. Maybe you grew up with adults telling you that you were special and powerful. Maybe you feel more like no one has ever truly believed in you, but you refuse to settle for mediocrity. There is a part of you that knows, *somehow*, that you don't have to be normal or average. A part of you that knows that you have *something* great within you, and you long for the opportunity to do something that really matters in this life. Either way, I have a special message for you:

You're right.

The truth is, you were born for nothing less than the greatest adventures you have ever dreamed of! You do not exist to live an average, dull, or even decently awesome life. You don't have to spend your time on earth struggling to get through each day or living for the weekends. You are unique and pricelessly powerful, regardless of past or present limitations. If you so choose, you can live your dream!

No, I'm not just writing this because it sounds inspirational. There is an art to figuring out what the heck to do with your life, and to skip over this point would be to seriously rip you off. The message of this chapter focuses on the part of your soul that wants to hope and pray and wish and daringly even believe that you are a hero born for greatness. I've taught many youth and young adults the process of finding their dream, but whether or not they understand the truths expressed in the next few pages is often a make-or-break point for them.

For some of you, this whole being a hero idea is a no brainer. You're getting pumped up by just remembering how great of a potential you know you have! For others, it might be a bit difficult, out of the ordinary, or even uncomfortable to believe what I'm saying and trust that you are a hero – especially when you consider all that idea means about you, your potential, and the responsibility you must take for your life.

If part of you is screaming "But Jacob, I'm NOT a hero, and if you knew me you would agree!" then don't freak out, and hold up just one minute. You've just gotta trust me for the next few pages, because this idea is critical for understanding the third step to discovering your dream and figuring out what you're supposed to do with your life.

So I repeat: the part of your soul that hopes and believes in your glorious destiny *is right*. YOU ARE A HERO. You *are* born to conquer mighty obstacles, you *are* destined to bless the lives of others in ways that no one else can, you *are* the master of your own fate, and you *are* capable of living the greatest, most fulfilling adventures.

You are a hero, so like every great story, yours can be filled with the opportunities that most people only hope for. If you actually understand it, this truth changes everything about how you'll live your life.

You are a hero.

And *because you are a hero*, you have a dream.

EVERY HERO NEEDS A DREAM

"I have a dream!" proclaimed Martin Luther King Jr. It was August 28, 1963, and on the steps of the Lincoln Memorial he proclaimed these now-famous words to a quarter of a million protesters on a hot summer afternoon. The dream he fought for was to lead his country to a new level of equality and justice. That dream was one of many dreams that has has changed the world.

Near the first half of the 15th century, a peasant girl named Joan of Arc confronted the royalty of France, led their armies into battle, and turned the tide of the Hundred Years War between her nation and the English. Her world-changing dream was to achieve freedom and peace for her people. Before being executed by her enemies at the young age of nineteen, she said of her dream "I am not afraid...I was born for this."

Steve Jobs championed a dream that changed our modern world, and if you want to know how, check your pocket. One of his most famous quotes goes like this: "Your work is going to fill a large part of your life, and the only way to be truly satisfied is to do what you believe is great work. And the only way to do great work is to love what you do." Do you think Jobs wanted to live the stereotypical life, or was he the type who dared to dream?

A critical part of my dream-education came from studying influential people from history, especially the ones I wanted to emulate. I read biographies, I had discussions with mentors and friends, and I wrote papers and articles on many such remarkable men and women. As I did so, I began to notice a peculiar and compelling pattern:

If you take a moment to look even briefly at their lives, you'll see that Martin Luther King Jr., Joan of Arc, Steve Jobs, and all the other revolutionary, inspired, powerful influencers who have made waves in history, *all had a dream*. They may not have called it by that name, but I challenge you to find me a single world-changer who wasn't driven by a meaningful purpose and clear direction on what they wanted to do with their lives.

Think about people from Alexander the Great to Mother Teresa, Christopher Columbus to Amelia Earhart, Thomas Jefferson to Arnold Schwarzenegger, and thousands more. Can you imagine great influencers like them *without* a dream? Look at Steve Jobs for example: who would he be without a dream? My guess is that he'd be a college dropout who people couldn't stand to work with, probably in a low paying job he hated or sleeping on the floor somewhere. We never would have heard of any of these people had they not been driven by a dream. They would have been nobodies!

So what makes these people stand out from the average Joe? It sure isn't circumstances of birth that enable people to make a great difference in our world. Truthfully, more often than not, our icons – our heroes – began with very little. Martin Luther King Jr. belonged to a grossly underprivileged minority, Joan of Arc was on the very bottom of a feudal pecking order, and Steve Jobs was an average college kid who didn't know what he wanted to do with his life. These heroic achievers were anything but privileged prodigies; they started out just like the rest of us!

But there IS at least one thing that these heroes found and embraced that enabled them to do more for the world than their circumstances would predict. One thing that drove them to radically exploit their potential. One thing more powerful than money, fame, or opportunity. What set these heroes apart was their dream.

As you know by now, when I refer to the dreams that set our heroes apart from the rest of humanity, I'm not talking about the "dream lifestyle". Wealth and fame are nice things to enjoy, but if they eclipse your dream, they drop to a caliber that simply doesn't do justice to the hero you are. Martin Luther King Jr., Joan of Arc, and Steve Jobs were not "living their dream" when they obtained a peak position of power, money, popularity, and relative ease – on the contrary, they only obtained those things as a step towards achieving their dream.

Your dream might lead millions to praise you, and might make you millions of dollars. It also might not. It won't matter though, because what it WILL give you is the ability to achieve a greatness that actually matters. Regardless of where your dream takes you, the point is this: *any who have ever achieved meaningful greatness or changed the world have done so in pursuit of a dream.*

Coincidence? I think not.

Now I know what you're thinking. Right about now you're looking at the handful of extraordinary achievers I listed and contemplating how they are totally the exceptions to the rule of normal-people-don't-change-the-world.

I'm not trying to say that you'll someday lead the armies of France because you wake up to a dream that says you will – although if that does happen to be your dream I truly believe that you can do so – I'm pointing out how the success of great people from history is inseparably intertwined with their dreams to teach you this truth:

You are a hero. Your dream will make you a better one.

There are many reasons why this is the case, but one of the greatest reasons why a dream is a critical path to becoming the greatest hero you can be is rooted in a very epic part of human nature. It's also the reason why I know for a fact that you have a dream in the first place.

Take a moment and think about the best stories you've ever heard, fictional or true. Think of superhero stories, fairy tales, parables, compelling moments from history class, biographies, news articles about inspiring people, and even the spastic story you told your friend about that exciting thing that happened to you yesterday.

Have you ever noticed that all the good stories follow the same pattern?

In his book, *A Hero With A Thousand Faces*, Joseph Campbell reviews hundreds of the most basic, fundamental stories – "myths" he calls them – that are told all over the world. He discovered a pattern that all interesting stories follow, which he calls The Hero Cycle. If you've ever taken a class on storytelling or creative writing, this probably sounds familiar to you.

The cycle goes something like this:

An ordinary, yet unique person is chillin' in a normal life, doing normal things. This person is the unsuspecting hero of the story.

Something extraordinary happens that shatters the status quo and inspires the hero to embark on a quest.

The hero accepts the call to adventure and, with the help of a mentor, steps into the unknown.

Many obstacles stand in the hero's way, leading up to a test so great that the hero fails many times and reaches their lowest moment before making a critical choice to try again.

The hero triumphs over the great obstacle, and with newfound strength proceeds to gain momentum and march towards victory and the accomplishment of his or her quest.

The quest is accomplished, the adventure completed, and the hero returns home to ordinary life – only this time the norm is much more awesome than it used to be and the hero is stronger and wiser than before.

The hero soon becomes accustomed to normal life, but it isn't long before something extraordinary happens that shatters the new status quo...

The reason this cycle shows up in every great story, and the reason it is so interesting to us, is because it is *our* story – it's a representation of the general pattern that every human being follows as we live, learn, and experience obstacles. If you've ever decided to do something new, got inspired by someone, faced setbacks, chose to not give up, and learned valuable lessons, then you've lived the Hero Cycle!

As you go through life, you'll face many such cycles. Some will take years for you to complete, and others will take a single day. Some will be relatively easy for you, others will take everything you've got. The greater the cycle, the greater the challenge, and the greater the reward.

What I want you to notice about this pattern, is that every revolution of it begins with a call to adventure; a moment when your familiar life is disrupted and you are inspired to venture into the unknown. Sometimes that call to adventure can come in the form of changing circumstances, such as people, opportunities, threats, or dire needs entering your life. But uncontrollable, external circumstances aren't the only kickstart to a new level of living. In fact, that type of call to adventure is actually very rare, especially when we're talking about the crazy big adventures that people tell stories about. I mean, when was the last time a sage guru knocked on your door, handed you a map and a magic sword, and told you the fate of the world rested on your shoulders?

Awesome? Definitely. Common? Not so much.

A lot of people are wasting away in their ordinary life, wishing they could go on adventures and fight battles and push their limits. They want an important quest to live, but they think they have to wait for something drastic to show up in their life. They metaphorically sit at home, gazing out the window as they wait for a life-changing call to adventure. It's not a very pleasant place to be in, because a hero without a challenge scarcely feels like a hero at all.

If this is you, don't worry. We've all been there before, and it's natural to wait for something to shake your world and tell you that greatness is within your grasp. That's exactly why I wrote this book. I'm calling you to adventure, because I know the secret that sets you uniquely and perfectly up for greatness:

You have a dream.

A truth that most people don't know, is that external circumstances aren't the only force that creates mind-blowing calls to adventure. You can wait all your life for things you can't control to kickstart your destiny, but you don't have to. There's a dream within you that will chart your course for the greatest, and most *real* journey you have ever imagined. In actuality, the pursuit of your dream is the only way to achieve lasting joy while embarking on the Hero Cycle – other motivations aren't strong enough alone (curiosity, the love of novelty and fun, etc) to pull you through the difficult times, or are negative at their core (revenge, survival, insecurity, etc.) and will ultimately leave you worn and broken. If you find your dream, it will kick you out your front door with the perfect call to adventure that you've been waiting for.

Are you seeing the beauty of this truth?

Heroes are grown through the journeys they go on. Just like the great men and women from your history books, if you want to max out your deepest potential, you need a dream to do so.

Does that mean that you're stuck in your progress because you don't have a dream? No! You are a hero. Heroes are built for dreams. You have a dream, and it's woven into your destiny. Your dream is part of you. You don't have to live in the normal and ordinary world a moment longer than you desire.

You picked up this book for a reason – because you were missing something in your life. You have a sense that you've outgrown the familiar world you live in, and you're ready for something big. The reason you feel this way is that you are a hero, and that means that you're not happy staying stagnant. You're looking for a dream because that is part of who you are.

Dreams and heroes are inseparably intertwined. One must have the other. It takes a hero to live a dream, and it takes a dream to make a hero.

So I ask you...how can there NOT be a dream for you?

To date I've taught literally hundreds of youth and young adults the information you read about in the last chapter. After I discovered what a dream was, I was launched into massive achievement and lit on fire about my life! Initially, I just assumed that the same thing would happen to everyone else who I could teach.

And my ranting and passionate jumping around on stage worked... for some people. But at the same time I would also have friends and students who would get inspired, want to find their dream, sometimes even come back to hear me speak over and over, but then never make significant progress in discovering or achieving their dream.

This observation was a mystery to me until I sat down to write this book. The reason why the truths about dreams impact some people more than others is provided for in taking the third step to discovering your dream. For most of my life I had simply taken this step for granted, and therefore not been able to see it. Discovering it was an incredibly fulfilling moment for me, because of the magnitude of how powerful it is.

The third step to finding your dream and figuring out what the heck to do with your life, is **Free The Hero Within.**

I always took being a hero for granted (I didn't always use that word, but I always believed that I was worthy of the greatest dreams that could come my way.) The truth is, not everyone feels that way. Sometimes situations shake our world, or the grind of long term difficulty wears away at us. Sometimes we simply forget who we are born to become. In those moments, it's tempting to choose to believe that we aren't good enough, strong enough, beautiful enough, worthy enough; that it's too hard, we're too young, too old, too inexperienced; that we are not loved, or not capable of loving…the list goes on.

It's easy to unconsciously accumulate identity garbage: some from what other people say to us and some from what we interpret in the midst of traumatic or disappointing circumstances. Maybe you've chosen to see yourself as unforgivable or unlovable because of mistakes you've made in the past. Maybe you've chosen to believe that no matter what you do, you have to be the type of hero who struggles on and on, never truly finding peace and joy. Maybe you've chosen to see yourself a background character, a victim in need of rescue, or even the villain in other people's stories.

These degrading, self-imposed identities result in a crippling lack of confidence and blindness to our own ability and truest desires. These types of beliefs about oneself aren't actually the truth, either – they are straight up lies that we breathe in and use to identify ourselves because we don't know any better.

We've all chosen to accept true things about ourselves, and also some limiting beliefs about who we are and what we are capable of – I guarantee that I've had my fair share of work to do in this area. As you live your life, you have the opportunity to remember more and more clearly each day the truth about who you have the potential to become. What you choose to believe about who you are will impact every facet of your life, and determine what quality of life you live.

The great part is that there's nothing you *have* to measure up to. You're at liberty to choose to believe in your heroic status on whatever level you want to! But if you want to find your dream, on the other hand, there is a minimum of heartfelt belief in yourself that you must choose to accept.

That's exactly what the third step is all about.

How can you live a BIG dream if you're too weak to leave what is comfortable?

How can you bring about a mighty change in the world if you don't have a powerful destiny?

How can you help others if you yourself are barely able to keep from drowning in your own problems?

How can you do good if you are not good?

How can you teach others to believe, if you live by doubt?

How can you walk the long path of a dream, if you're stuck and broken?

How can you live a dream, if you are less than a hero?

When you believe falsehoods about your worth and capacity, you bind yourself with unnecessary limitations. If you allow these limitations to grow and remain, they will cripple your journey towards discovering and living your dream because your beliefs fundamentally shift your perception and the actions you take. So ask yourself this: "What have I chosen to believe about myself that is not consistent with my truest and highest self?"

Among all gifts, powers, and tools that heroes like you and I are given to do great things with, a dream is among the top three most important. Along the way, your dream will shape the best you. But before you can be shaped, the real you has to show up! If you don't show up, your dream never can.

Ultimately, you will find that your dream is the perfect expression of who you are. That's why it's so powerful. That's why it's so needed. The more you learn who you are, and choose to embody your truest and highest self, the easier it will be to find your dream. When you choose to see your life as that of a hero, finding your dream becomes more or less inevitable.

Whatever identity garbage you have collected and held on to over the years, now is your time to reevaluate. It's *easy* to believe lies about our true potential and destiny, but no matter what you've chosen in the past, I'm inviting you in *this moment* to remember who you are. Forever and always, this truth remains: you are a hero. It takes a hero to live a dream; and it takes a dream to shape a hero.

As you choose to free the hero within, you must with solemnity and complete candor ask two soul-confronting questions:

1. "Am I worth it?"
2. "Do I have what it takes?"

These are most often the two greatest barriers to a hero becoming free and finding his or her dream. You will know that you have sufficiently freed the hero within you enough to discover your dream when you answer yes to both questions.

AM I WORTH IT?

At one of my very first speaking events (I'll let you take one guess at what I was presenting on), I remember meeting a young woman sitting in the front row. Her name is Rylee, and she has a dream. We recently reconnected, and she, now eighteen years old, shared with me her dream "To help women discover their true worth through writing and speaking."

When I asked her how she discovered her dream, I was amazed to learn to what extent she had wrestled with the heart wrenching question, "Am I worth it?"

"It was a long hard process for me," she related. "I had to go through a time where I felt worthless. It started from the time I was young, but it got worse as soon as I hit my teens. I didn't really have any friends, which made me feel like there was something wrong with me because I wasn't being accepted."

Rylee shared with me how her desire to be accepted led her to change who she knew she was to fit in with others. She changed how she dressed, the movies and music she consumed, and how she acted. "But month after month and year after year, the only thing that changed was me. And it wasn't for the better," she continued.

"I still wasn't being accepted, which led to me feeling even worse about myself and getting really depressed. So I began looking for attention from guys. I thought it would make me feel worth more if a guy liked me. Well, this only led to trouble. I got attention from guys, but they were not good guys and they all tried to take advantage of me at some point. They didn't treat me like a person, they treated me like an object." At this her lowest point, Rylee did not see her own heroic worth.

Have you ever believed that the person that you are isn't worth much? Or have you ever believed that you're not good enough or worthy enough for love? Have your doubts about your worth ever driven you to trade your personal values or attributes for acceptance by others? Regardless of whether you've been in a situation similar to Rylee's low point or not, you will someday face the temptation to conclude that who you are on the inside isn't worth greatness, a dream, or the life of a hero.

This is a dream-smothering inclination because if you don't believe you're good enough for a dream, you won't be able to see it when it shows up. Your dream is the perfect expression of who you are, so for it you be *your dream,* you need to be *you.* If you deny your values and attributes to become someone else, you will also deny the dream which highlights and enables your best self.

As for Rylee, her turning point came when she was seventeen:

"I decided I was done trying to be someone else," she said. After making this choice, Rylee began to surround herself with people who reminded her of her worth and encouraged her to find her unique mission in life. A short time later she discovered just how important it was that she claimed her worth: "I discovered that helping others discover their worth was my mission, because I wanted to help prevent other girls from going through what I went through."

Like Rylee, you must choose to accept and nurture the confidence that you are beyond worth it. You have a dream, and if you want to find it, you must first find you.

DO I HAVE WHAT IT TAKES?

Daniel, a young man with an incredible dream, didn't always believe that he had what it took. When he was twelve he discovered his immense passion for physical fitness, and threw himself into it with everything he had, sensing that what he wanted to do with his life would involve his newfound love. He converted his room into a gym, took martial arts, threw himself into numerous fitness programs, and trained for many hours a day.

Everything changed for him one morning when he woke up to a body that wouldn't move. Seemingly out of nowhere, any physical motion caused him extraordinary levels of joint pain. The doctors had no idea what was wrong with him! Over the next few months he resigned himself to limping around his house in constant pain, dropping out of school, and sinking deeper and deeper into depression. His already lean body would lose thirty pounds of muscle.

For a hero with a deep passion for physical fitness and movement, can you imagine a more devastating situation? In the midst of his suffering, Daniel remembers a specific moment in which he gave up on his dream, deciding that he couldn't do it:

"It was the most devastatingly crushing feeling I've ever experienced," he told me. "For a couple years my life persisted, but I was wandering, seemingly hopelessly, in the darkness. My confidence was nonexistent. My passion was dead. I was utterly miserable."

This life was Daniel's reality for an entire three years. He would later learn that his joint pain was his body's physical expression of a depression that began as a result of a school situation in which he felt overwhelming frustration and inadequacy for an extended period of time. His healing came the day that he chose to free the hero he had locked away for protection. When Daniel speaks of this transformative moment, he refers to it as his Miracle.

On an evening in April he was sitting alone in a movie theater, listening to the music as the credits rolled by. In spite of his hopeless stupor, he had limped himself across the street from the LA hotel his family was staying the night in. As he sat in the after-movie darkness, pondering, something began to change within him.

"What am I so afraid of?" He asked himself. Tears streamed down his face, and he contemplated the shell of a life driven by hate and hopelessness that he was living.

"Pain," he realized. "I'm afraid of pain."

"But wait a minute," Daniel thought, "I've been living in constant pain for three years!"

It was then that Daniel made a choice that would finally set him free: as the music played on in the dark theater, he chose to pull down the walls layer by layer that had created his prison and silenced his dream. As he reached out to his Maker, Daniel chose to soften his heart and, once again, choose to believe. His broken soul was picked up and put back together piece by piece in a moment of divine healing. Within three minutes, the physical pain he had suffered for the last three years was gone for good.

"...I realized that my Dream was still possible," he recalled of that moment. "I thought I had lost it, but in fact it had only been buried. This time I consciously decided that I would live my dream, no matter how hard it might get, and I would never, ever give up on it again."

Daniel walked out of that theater a changed man. He faced a long road ahead of him to regain his physical fitness, social skills, and to catch up on the years of school work he had missed. But finally, he knew he had what it took to face any obstacle life could throw at him. He had chosen to free the hero within himself, and the roots of his dream began to grow again.

In the year after his Miracle, Daniel's passion rapidly expanded into a very big dream: Upon This Rock Fitness Center, a fitness gym unlike any other on the planet. He loves physical fitness, but also wants to help people achieve mental, financial, emotional, and spiritual fitness. He passionately describes in detail a gym in which you enter not only to pump iron, but to grow yourself into the best person you can possibly be. In a sentence, Daniel's dream is "To lead the human race to a higher state of freedom through fitness."

Daniel is currently training to win the Crossfit Games and the title of "fittest man on earth." When I asked him how a dream has impacted his life, he replied: "My dream has given me great clarity and personal power in my life. I know what I want, which gives me the ability to better discern between the right opportunities for me. I live each day with intention and make meaningful progress on a regular basis. My passion and enthusiasm for life is also radically enhanced. My dream gives me immeasurable hope for the future."

I share Daniel's story because if you don't believe you have what it takes to achieve your dream and do it justice, *it won't matter if you find it or not.* If you don't believe you have what it takes to live your dream, you'll either give up on it entirely or tuck it away somewhere safe until it decays into nothingness.

If you have doubts about whether or not you have the capacity to do something truly great, than, like Daniel, you must realize that life is preparing you in all necessary ways for victory over the obstacles your dream will uncover. In fact, you're the ONLY person who will ever have everything it takes to live YOUR dream. That's why it belongs to you!

It's natural to feel inadequate and unprepared when faced with the possibility of living a great and glorious dream. You might not feel ready. You might not feel worthy. But one of the greatest truths I know about dreams is that if your dream has shown up, it means that you're ready – even though you're not perfect. You will never be fully qualified to live your dream, but you'll always be fully capable.

Of course you have weaknesses, but so does every other hero this world produces! Yes, there are many things that you'll have to learn along the way, but you can't afford to allow your present weaknesses to limit your very real and powerful potential for achievement. Choose to soften your heart and trust the part of you that desires to believe that yes, you do have what it takes. Don't be afraid of what you are not; embrace and find power in what you *are*!

Your moment of transformation might not turn out as extreme as Daniel's did, and hopefully you haven't had to go through the pain that he did to learn your true strength and capability to achieve your dream. When you do find your freedom, however, you will finally be able to see the dreams and desires that are calling your name.

FREEING THE HERO WITHIN

To free the hero within, you must alter the beliefs you hold about yourself such that you can fully accept your value, ability, and irreplaceability. You must rid yourself of any monsters inside your head that tell you you aren't good enough, worthy enough, or capable enough for wild success, for living a life of incredible adventure and meaning, for a world-changing dream, and a host of other good things. You will not be free to discover or live the greatness of your dream until you choose to see and embrace the greatness within *you*.

Now I must be clear here: seeing your own greatness has nothing to do with being fully qualified to live your dream. If it did, we wouldn't be able to see our personal worth until after we've completed our dream, if ever. Remember Martin Luther King Jr., Joan of Arc, and Steve Jobs? When they set out to live their dreams, they were far from prepared or remotely qualified. At the same time, they were perfect for their heroic roles. They didn't allow their inadequacies to overpower them, and that willingness to embark on the journey combined with their unique gifts, talents, and future potential made them capable of success.

Often, the biggest dreams are given to heroes who appear grossly unqualified. When faced with the magnitude of my own dream, I can personally vouch for that idea: when I set out to find my dream, I was in no way ready to accomplish it. There are still days when I have to admit that I have *no idea* what I'm doing. Like, none. Nada. Thankfully, that doesn't matter. The belief that you are good enough to get started is the only requirement.

You will know you're on the right track when you can in joyful sincerity say that you love yourself. You'll know when you look in the mirror one day and realize that you can't *not* achieve greatness in life – who you are will not permit anything less. You'll know when you don't have the slightest problem declaring to the world that you are a hero and accepting everything that entails; the fear and pain, the direction and inspiration, the victory and love.

Perhaps most of all, you'll know you're getting it when you start to take action. Not just the same sort of action that you're used to living, but new action that honors the best that you are. Action is a natural result of our deepest beliefs. The more free you become, the faster your life changes into more of what you want. When you begin believing something different about who you are, the results that you create in your life simultaneously begin to shift.

As it turns out, one of the best ways to reinforce new and useful beliefs, is to take action. Together, choice of action and choice of belief will create a powerful pattern of progress. If you find yourself in a slump where you "know" intellectually that you're a hero with immense potential, but are having a day (or year!) where it seems like nothing's going right or that you're just in a constant state of "bleh" with no motivation, then alongside your shift in belief, you need to do something crazy to wake yourself up.

To get you started, here are some of the things I've done to get out of those low moments:

- Take an ice cold shower (crying is okay, chickening out is not).
- Run a mile. Or 10. Or a marathon in the middle of the night down an empty canyon.
- Delete that app that sucks your life away. Your know the one.
- Pour your bottle of Hershey's syrup down the drain (alas, my achilles heel).
- Initiate a conversation with family member about what you're going through.
- Throw your TV off a cliff. (Alternatively, sell it on eBay).
- Binge watch motivational videos on YouTube.
- Text a wise guru figure in your life.
- Clean the mess of a place you call your room (I've been there).

These sorts of actions can kickstart your life, and are very useful. But the motivation you get from them won't last long unless you make a fundamental choice to believe something different about who you are.

In the story of your life, you are both the jailer and the prisoner. If the hero within you is not free, it is because, somewhere along the way, you have chosen it. That can be hard to hear, but the beautiful thing is that if you can choose to be bound, you can also choose to be free. And you can do it now.

No matter who you are or what you've done, you always have a choice.

If you want to discover and accomplish your dream, you must choose to set free the hero within you. A hero is your natural state. Anything else is a mask that you've chosen to hide behind.

You have a divine identity. Your choice in this moment is whether you will rise to it.

Choose to let love overcome your fear.

Choose to let faith strengthen your weaknesses.

Choose to eradicate your worry and doubt.

Choose to stand boldly against your greatest trials.

Choose to accept with joy the magnitude of your potential.

Choose to believe that your are a hero, nothing less!

If you have been hurt from the past, it's time for you to forgive, heal your heart, and let go of what you cannot change.

If you feel that circumstance is holding you back, know that you can rise above any circumstance. If you feel trapped, your freedom will come by knowing that you hold the keys to your deliverance.

If you've been looking for someone to give you permission to become a hero and let the world see the greatness within you, then let me be your champion today: I give you permission to be magnificent, powerful, and heroic beyond any earthly expectations.

But you never needed that permission anyways, because you're a hero. A *freakin' hero!*

To the end of freeing the hero within on a daily basis, I have designed two practical tools for you to use. I use both of these tools every single day, and I've been using variations of them for years. I can't stress enough how effective and worth your time they are, so you'll just have to trust me and try them out for yourself.

TOOL #1: AFFIRMATIONS - Create a list of the most empowering personal beliefs you can think of. Write them in a form that is positive, present, and powerful ("I am brilliant", "I love my life", "I take action easily and effortlessly", "I'm a hero", etc.) Spend 5 minutes every morning repeating this list to yourself with as much energy as you can. By doing so consistently, you will find your mind filled more and more with these phrases. Soon enough, you'll find it easy to believe in them and in your own potential.

TOOL #2: ASK AND ACT - Begin by putting yourself into a good emotional state (move your body, exercise, repeat affirmations, have a solo dance party, etc.) Then, close your eyes, take a deep, grounding breath. Ask yourself this question: "How do I get to honor the hero within me today?" The first answer that lights into your mind is the one to trust. Open your eyes, write your answer down, and take immediate action on it.

Remember that you always have a choice. You are a hero, so it's time you lived like one. It will take nothing less than a hero to live the adventure that is your dream; good thing you just so happen to be the perfect one for the task!

In your Dream Journal, reflect on and answer these three questions by writing a letter to yourself:

What do you see in your favorite heroes (historical, fiction, living now) that you want to also see in yourself?

How have you been holding yourself back from living like a hero would?

What is your true potential and greatness?

The 7 Steps to Discovering Your Dream:

1. CHOOSE TO SEEK YOUR DREAM

If you want to find your dream, you need to deliberately search for it. Make the intentional choice to become a dreamer. Naysayers will call this process risky, but the greatest risk is never living at your highest potential. Decide that the answer to what YOU want to do with your life will be found by discovering your dream.

2. KNOW WHAT YOU'RE LOOKING FOR

The more clearly you can define what you want, the more direct your path to obtaining it will be. Study the principles and formulas that characterize dreams. Write out your life purpose. Reflect on your passions, aptitudes, and the needs of the world. Take the time to decide how you'll know YOUR dream when you find it.

3. FREE THE HERO WITHIN

You can't find your dream until you have taken responsibility for your life. It takes a hero to live a dream. Choose to learn of, and believe in, your divine worth and potential. Stop holding yourself back. Instead, give yourself permission to be great.

FOUR

MOUNTAINS TO CLIMB

What we obtain too cheap, we esteem too lightly; it is dearness only that gives everything its value.
~ Thomas Paine

Have you ever had your life changed by a single conversation?

I still remember the text message conversation responsible for kicking off the dream behind Lionheart Mentoring – and the inevitable next step towards me discovering and living my dream. It was about 10:30 at night, and I was laying in my bed. My thumbs were chatting away, probably with a pretty girl.

The year was drawing to a close, and it had been over 8 months since Celine and I had gotten fired up about the youth in the world who needed to understand their potential, and set to work writing articles and trying to spread the word about them. The blog was going okay, but it wasn't exactly changing the world. Or anyone, it felt like.

That's when I got a text from Quiana.

Quiana is a 5'1" girl, a year older than I am. She's got the mind of a brilliant storyteller and an indomitable spirit. I knew Quiana because we volunteered together on a youth committee tasked with creating week-long educational simulations for teenagers. The simulations were pretty cool, except that somehow, I always ended up playing the role of a psychopath or evil military henchman. I'm still trying to figure out why that happened and what it means for my future.

"I've been thinking," Quiana's text read. "I really want to become a public speaker and go to schools and inspire youth with positive messages. Wouldn't that make such a big difference? They have so much potential, and we know principles that they need to live by. I thought I'd reach out to you because I know that you're interested in that sort of thing."

"That's awesome!" I replied. "I love that, and that's totally part of my dream." She was definitely talking to the right person. After a conversation about our shared passion for how badly the youth in our world needed to hear our messages of high expectations, virtue, and empowerment, I threw out a question she didn't expect:

"So do you want to do it?"

"Wait. Like, now?" she hesitated.

"Yeah, let's do this now!"

"Uh, yeah. Alright then. Okay. Yes. Why not?"

And that, my friends, is how to launch into the next step of your dream – with reckless commitment after a few minutes of semi-attentive consideration. No, it doesn't always happen like that, but in this instance, we both felt that this was a great idea that would directly enable us to achieve our dreams.

The next day we had a brainstorming session, and decided to title our project with the most spirited name we could come up with... Lionheart Discourse.

We envisioned ourselves doing school assemblies, speaking to youth groups and organizations, and all around being some chill, inspirational role models. That was basically all we envisioned at that point. We didn't even want to do anything related to mentoring youth – the very thing we are now known for. The idea of coaching and teaching people as well as presenting on stage didn't enter the picture until we pitched the idea to our fellow radical-world-changer, and my best friend, Dallin. He wanted in on our adventure, but on two conditions: he could focus on mentoring people, and we had to change the name.

Thank you, Dallin. Thank you.

If only we could have known then where our shared dream would take us, our jaws would have dropped. It wasn't just results that we ended up with, though we got plenty of those too. Perhaps the most unexpected, yet profoundly beneficial thing that we ended up with through our pursuit of this daring adventure was a bigger, clearer, more compelling dream.

When we were first starting out, our shared dream could basically be summed up like this: "Inspire and teach youth that they can do incredible things with their lives." A year later, after dozens of dead ends, failed projects, and a handful of joyous successes, our shared dream looked like this: "Change the world of youth forever by championing a movement of speaking, mentoring, and leadership among western civilization, designed to teach youth that they have a divine identity, they have a unique and priceless purpose, and that no matter their circumstances they can choose to be free."

Quite the upgrade, isn't it?

Even to this day, we are constantly re-evaluating our direction, finding clarity on exactly what we are being called to do with this incredible dream. Knowing clearly what we want to accomplish gives us immense power to do so. That clarity didn't show up right from day one, *even though we were actively living our dream*.

In the beginning, all we had was a mess of inspiration to do *something* like what our dream actually ended up being. We just knew that we wanted to get messages of truth and empowerment out to our peers because we saw that they desperately needed it.

So within a few days of our fateful text conversation, we had put together our first speaking gig for about twenty five youth. We then spoke to a class at a high school because Quiana had connections with one of the teachers. After that, we spoke to a group of youth at a small private school. We didn't know exactly what we were doing, but our vague dream was all we needed.

Months later, in a deep brainstorming and strategy session, we created a mission statement. Finally, we knew, (kind of what) our organization was all about. We also decided that a movement was the only way to enact the change we wanted to see in the world, and we created a long-term strategy to bring it international within a few years.

A short time later, we created an official business organization to help us have credibility and gain leverage in organizing events (because most people don't want to sell event insurance to a seventeen year old. Go figure.) We realized that there wasn't a chance of us changing the world all on our own, so we hired a team, gathered volunteers, and began training other youth to be mentors and speakers.

Another couple of months passed by, and we finally sat down and decided which core principles would be the main focus of our movement. Typically, it's a bad idea to wait six months into a project before deciding what to focus on, but we didn't have enough clarity and experience to answer that question before then, so we acted on what we had at the time. Months later, we again fine tuned those principles, and our dream became clearer.

I share this story about our dream because firstly, it's awesome and rare enough to be proudly akin to a unicorn. Sadly, it just isn't common for teenagers to do things like what we did, because even though they are extremely powerful and capable, most of them either don't know it, or they don't know what they should do with all that potential – which is exactly why Lionheart exists, and why I wrote this book!

Secondly, this story illustrates a profound truth about dreams. Most people who look for their dream are held back by an idea I like to call the Myth of One-Time-Dream-Discovery:

Living a dream is like climbing a mountain, and this myth says that you'll be able to start living your dream once you can stand at the bottom and look up an intimidating, yet straight path up a clean mountain face and see exactly where you want to be and the general path to get there. The myth says that your dream is a happy sanctuary of knowledge which you have to search and search to obtain, but that once you've obtained it, the rest is purely a matter of grit, persistence, and determination as you climb upward. That's what the myth says, and the myth isn't entirely true.

The truth is that the path up the mountain of your dream leads through valleys, ravines, rivers, and canyons. There are many paths to the summit, but none of them are straight or clear. Fog and trees often block your view, and the only thing you can clearly see is the trail directly ahead of you...until it bends around a hill. The path of your dream not a place for a casual walk in the park; it's more like the perfect location for a great adventure.

A truth that dispels the Myth of One-Time-Dream-Discovery is that the only place you'll see *perfectly* what your dream looks like is when you've reached the summit – and by that point, you've already achieved your dream!

This means that as you seek out and climb the mountain of your dream, you will occasionally find yourself stuck in holes that you don't think you can get out of, you will have days when you'll be completely exhausted from your search, and there will be times when your view of the next step you need to take is blocked by a thicket of metaphorical trees.

There will also be moments along the journey when the going is easy and you can see for miles ahead of you – when you obtain a new vision of the success of your dream, the next steps, or upcoming challenges. In these moments, it will feel as if you've climbed to the top of a cliff, and can suddenly behold a long valley ahead; or as if the ground has risen sharply before you, unhindered by obstacles, and you can clearly see how to continue your climb

As you take steps towards your dream, you will naturally be enabled to see further and with more clarity. Your sight will expand every day that you move towards your destination. Sometimes in small steps, other times in grand strides.

The idea that you're going to find your dream all at once keeps a lot of people wandering around the base of their mountain, never climbing because they're worried that they don't know exactly where they are headed. You might be one of these people. You might also be one of the people way back in their living room, sorting through the maps of "higher education" because they don't even know what mountain they want to climb in the first place!

Either way, I'm about to share with you a truth that will help you as you take the fourth step to discovering your dream and figuring out what the heck to do with your life:

Finding your dream is a journey, not a one-time event.

To be honest, I wouldn't have it any other way. I consider it a blessing that we can't dig up the entire roadmap before we get started. Life would be too boring for heroes like you and I if we had all the answers all the time. We are heroes worthy of being tried and tested. To live a propper adventure, we need uncertainty and confusion as much as we need certainty and vision. That's why we get so upset at a friend who spoils a highly anticipated movie.

Not only does this truth heighten the adventure, but I believe that if we fully understood the actual difficulty and magnitude of impact that our dreams involved from day one, we wouldn't be so quick to get inspired. There's a high chance we would be too scared or hesitant, too overwhelmed to get started in the first place. The full vision would look like a LOT of work, a LOT of responsibility, and a LOT of success that we aren't ready for!

When you picked up this book, did you think that finding your dream would be a one-time even? Did you think that you were going figure out what you were going to do with your life, once and for all, and be done with it? I've been fooled by the myth plenty of times myself. But just ask any experienced dreamer, and they'll probably laugh and tell you that they've had to figure out what they wanted to be when they grew up many times over.

The next step to finding your dream points out why you probably won't read this book, ponder for a few hours, and then walk away with an understanding of the full magnitude of your dream and the path to achieve it. I mean, it could happen (in which case, please contact me with the good news), but I'm willing to bet that what you'll discover instead will be far more valuable to you.

What you *will* find, is the beginning of a path that calls your soul forward. It might look like a purpose at first. Perhaps a passion. A better version of yourself. Maybe a very important goal. From there, as you take action and dedicate your focus to accomplishing your dream, your clarity will continue to grow and grow. The road ahead is fraught with new insights and possibilities, waiting for you to uncover and learn from them one step at a time. Your dream will be found on the road you take to live it.

Now, this doesn't mean that you should stop looking for a dream altogether because you'll never "figure it out" anyways; this does not mean that any road you take is the right one. HECK TO THE NO, DUDE! What it means is that if your full dream hasn't shown up at your doorstep yet, you won't help your case by sitting around and waiting for it. In fact, sitting around and waiting for your dream to show up is one of the most effective ways to completely defeat the mission you are called to achieve.

"Well, I'm screwed then," You might be thinking. "I don't even know what my dream is in the first place, so stop throwing around paradoxical statements about how I need to live it before I can find it!"

Never fear. I have come prepared for this situation.

The parts of your dream you haven't discovered yet will, indeed, be found as you act upon what you already have. The blessedly good news is that in right now you already have all the information you need in order to move towards your dream, even if it's only in a small way! If your full dream isn't standing on your doorstep, the you need to realize that *part* of your dream is standing right next to you. It's the start of the path; a first step, even if that step feels blind.

Look back at your Dream Journal. How can you take action based on what you have already written there? What interests, desires, and opportunities could get you closer to your dream? What is that one thing that you haven't faced yet, but that you know you've been meaning to for a long time?

If you're still insisting that you have no idea where to go even after you've looked through your notes, try this exquisitely subtle strategy: SHUT UP AND STOP IT. Stop telling yourself that you don't know what your dream is, and instead, listen to the fragments of a dream that are already inside of you, no matter how small, random, or seemingly unrelated they may be. Stop giving power to your lack of direction by insisting that you don't have a dream.

You *do* have a dream, and it's closer to you than you might think. You just have to stop talking, stop insisting, and stop worrying. Rather than focusing on what you don't know, choose to trust what you do know.

Take a minute to ask yourself the following question, then write your answer in your Dream Journal: "How can I take action on what I already know about my dream?"

There have been many times in my life where a profound experience unveils a new side of my dream. There have also been many *more* moments where I've learned bits and pieces, almost daily, as I go along. Your moment of massive realization will come, but only after you've proven that you can handle the steps that you already have. It's time for you to begin the journey towards your dream whether you feel ready or not. It's time for you to take your next step!

The fourth step to discovering your dream and figuring out what the heck to do with your life is **Pay The Price For Your Dream**.

The way you pay this price is simple: Take action. Move, even if you're not 100% sure where to. Step out your front door and just start walking towards your dream. No matter where you currently are, it's your job to get up and get going.

Paying the price is a critical step for many reasons, but one of the greatest is that it proves that you are a hero who cares enough about having a dream to do it justice once you obtain it. In the words of founding-era American author Thomas Paine, "What we obtain too cheap we esteem too lightly." A dream is a precious gift, not to be handed out carelessly. It is your privilege to fight for and claim yours.

You will know that you have sufficiently paid the price for your dream when you walk into an opportunity that makes your goals tangible and your vision concrete. You'll know you've paid the price when you step into a new arena of life and see a specific possibility that compels you to joyfully exclaim "That's it! I can do that. I *must* do that. I was born for this!" That's the golden moment you're looking for. Along the way, you'll have similar moments on a smaller scale, which serve as an indicator to you that you're headed in the right direction.

One of my close friends and fellow mentor at Lionheart, Ashlie, has been paying the price for her dream faster than most heroes I know. At age eighteen and with a break from school she in the perfect place to charge in the direction of her dream.

Ashlie and I were driving home one night after an event, when she suddenly turned to me and declared that she had just discovered the next big step towards her dream!

"And the great part is," she said, "That last night I broke down and was crying on my floor because I couldn't figure it out." She followed that up with a characteristic laugh, and I started taking notes.

Over the previous half dozen months, Ashlie had often talked about her dream. Up until recently, she saw her dream this way: "To bring people closer to their wholeness through diet, exercise, healing and personal character." That was the purpose that drove her forward and gave her direction. It served her for a time, and led her to serve others in powerful ways and become a better hero in the process.

About a week before our car ride, however, one of her friends asked Ashlie a few deep, inspired questions about her dream. These questions sent Ashlie into a life-purpose tailspin akin to that of an airplane that suddenly has one of it's wings chopped off mid-flight. Ashlie realized that while her current understanding of her dream was close to what she wanted to do with her life, it was no longer close enough.

This friend continued to mentor her with questions, and Ashlie desperately sought for new clarity. Ashlie told me that, under the new pressure of inquiry, she watched her out-dated understanding of her dream "fall apart, and crumble and die."

"What wasn't real disappeared," she said. It had served her up until this point, and now she was ready for something more.

So with heroic determination, Ashlie paid the price for the next level of her dream. She asked people – almost everyone in her life – what they thought. She counseled with mentors and friends. She reviewed and applied the Big Dream Formula. She stayed up late mapping her thoughts out on her whiteboard. She looked up jobs online, searching for what might interest her. She wrote lists and lists and more lists.

One night she had a breakdown. "Crying on the floor and breaking down set me up to figure it out," She said. "It didn't feel great at the time, but as soon as I figured it out, I was like…[fist pump with bubbly laugh of happiness]."

Nothing clicked for Ashlie until the next evening, when in a moment of peaceful reflection, she asked herself a simple question: "What is my next step?"

The answer came immediately. *Learn to love yourself.*

As Ashlie described it, she immediately identified this as what was missing. For her, it was the purpose that rallied all the other pieces together. With all the pieces together in one unified puzzle, Ashlie could (finally) see the picture of what it looked like.

"My dream is to teach people that they have a purpose, a reason to live, a mission to pursue!" Ashlie enthusiastically told me as we drove. "I dream of sharing that message...I don't have it super specific yet, but I know there will be events, a book, discussions, online material, and mentoring."

Ashlie had discovered the next level of her dream! When I asked her what role the effort she expended played in the discovery of her dream, she triumphantly dropped this truth: "Crying on the floor of your bedroom is the moment when you realize that you have to have it at any cost to yourself. It's the moment you realize it has to be yours. It's the passion. It's the pain. And it's the acceptance of the blood, sweat, and tears that are going to get you there."

Ashlie's story illustrates that not only will there come to you a moment of breakthrough where your dream becomes drasticly clearer, but that they way to get to that place is to take step four with gusto – emphasis on the gusto.

You can pay the price for your dream quickly or slowly; you can choose to charge towards the unknown, or you can take your time and see what life brings you. I've seen people do it both ways, and I'm not here to tell you what approach is better for you. All I want you to know right now is that if you're stuck without a dream and it's frustrating you to no end because you need your dream to give you direction and supercharge the hero that you are, you don't have to sit around and wait. You can run towards your dream with fire and determination, and doing so will shorten the time that your process of paying the price requires. The bold approach is exactly what enabled me to find my dream at such a relatively young age!

So if you've always wanted to do something, do it! If there's something new in your life that you guess might have the potential to be interesting, try it! If you know you need to work on something in your life, get help! Those steps may look big, and they may look small. The steps you take to discover and live your dream aren't always equal, but each one has been placed before you for a reason. You won't get more clarity until you take responsibility for what you already have.

The dream that I have today developed over a year and a half of dedicated work, guided by a dream to teach youth from the stage. That dream came after 8 months of working on a blog with the dream to inspire youth to reach for their true potential. And THAT dream came a full year after I discovered that I eventually wanted to become a public speaker and writer, during which I, based on my future vision, spent the year getting into college, building a small business, and practicing my oratory skills.

I've paid the price for my dream. So has Ashlie and thousands of other heroes just like you. We agree that it is so very, very worth it.

Now, it's your turn.

THE DREAM GROWTH CYCLE

There is a simple process – a cycle of action – that I have used over and over to pay the price for my dream. I challenge you to find any mentor or dreamer you respect and ask them if following the process below will help you figure out what to do with your life. My bet is that they will nod their head and say "Yes, you should absolutely do that." Why? Because it's very likely that, intentionally or not, they used the same process in some form or another when searching for their dream.

If you aren't positive where to begin searching for your dream, this cycle will guide you to the type of action that you need next. If you already have an idea of what your dream is, this cycle will give you an understanding of the process of discovering further clarity as you continue to pay the price for your dream.

Learning the three phases of this cycle is like learning to walk: critical if you want to avoid moving towards your dream at the speed of crawling. But just as important as this process is, it must be used alongside an adequate knowledge of what you're looking for (step number two). Otherwise you'll travel and travel, never knowing what exactly you're looking for. If you use the two strategies together, you'll drive towards your dream with a nearly unstoppable force.

Tie your shoes and study the following three phases of action. Apply the one you need most, move to the next, the next, and then loop back to the beginning and start over until the dreamer in your heart screams "YES, I'VE FOUND IT!"

PHASE 1 - EXPLORATION

Try new things, meet new people, and have new experiences. Explore the world around you in breadth, and dive deeper into the areas that your clues have lead you to.

Have you ever wanted to visit far away places in the world? I hear people talk all the time about how they want to "travel the world" someday. Some of them will even tell you that doing so is their dream! For 99% of these people, I don't actually think their dream is to travel the world. Rather, what they are experiencing is a call to move towards their dream by searching for new paths they have never considered. There's a little voice inside of them telling them that their next step is to go explore so they can find something better for their lives; a greater dream that they haven't even touched yet!

If you've never found something that you love doing with all your heart, or something that you're exceptionally gifted at, or a problem in the world that really needs to be solved, it doesn't mean those things don't exist. It just means you've never experienced them before! Would Mozart have lived his dream as a world famous composer if he had never heard an orchestra or picked up a violin?

Of course not! In fact, he probably would have lived his whole life feeling like a failure.

At the age of sixteen, when I started telling people that I had been accepted to BYU, most of them were shocked. They were shocked because they didn't know that was something that the average person could do! Up until the year before, I actually didn't either. Before I ever set a goal to be admitted to college early, my mind had been similarly blown by one of my role models:

We were at was at a surprise birthday party for a mutual friend, when my buddy, Quinton, started catching me up on his life. I asked him where he was going to school. In his characteristic casual confidence, he said something along the lines of "I just started college at George Wythe University..."

I did a double take and my mind crunched numbers about our small age difference.

"And you're, what, sixteen years old?" I asked.

"Oh yeah, it's cool," Quinton smiled as he casually dismissed the relevance of age.

Huh, I mused. *People do stuff like that?*

"You should do it too," he continued. "I think you could do it."

"That's awesome! Who knows, maybe I will." I replied, and the conversation drifted elsewhere.

You know what, Quinton? You're right...I can do that, and I think I'm going to.

Had I never been exposed to the possibility of taking a different path to education than the norm, I highly doubt I ever would have chosen to. It's the moments of exploration that give you the words you need to write your destiny.

Some moments of exploration come into your life unexpectedly, such as my conversation with Quinton. But for the rest of your exploration moments – the ones in which you need to go deliberately explore the world – there are two roles that you should embody in different phases of discovering your dream. You'll be able to figure out which role you need to play based on how much of your dream you already understand and how much you still need to figure out.

One role is that of the **Adventurer**. The adventurer goes out into the wide world and tries as many new things as possible. He or she is studying astronomy one day, playing the tuba the next day, and fighting in an MMA rink the next. Sometimes you just have to go out and get a physical grip on a subject, but one of the best ways to explore is to read books; I've read hundreds of books throughout my teenagehood (literally, I've kept count), and very few of them were required by a class. Exposure to great ideas will exponentially expand your understanding of what your dream could look like. Overall, when adventuring, shoot for *breadth* of exploration with the goal of experiencing maximum diversity.

The other role is that of the **Detective**. The detective comes into play when you've found something that you think has a high potential for being a major passion, aptitude, or need in the world. Once you've been clued into such a subject, activity, or group of people, it's time to figure out what exactly it is about the experience that speaks to you. The best way to do that is to dig deeper and investigate related experiences, as well as the lives of the people who have found their dream there. For example, let's say you really enjoy stage acting. If you interview actors and participate in a production, you might realize that it's the working with people that you really love, and that you don't care so much for actually saying the lines. Perhaps then you would realize that you also love creating stories – next thing you know, you're the director of the show! As you experiment with *depth*, you will soon discover valuable gems of what your dream should include.

If you don't have very many good ideas for what your dream might include, or you feel like the ideas you do have are noticeably underwhelming, then exploring is the phase for you to dive into.

PHASE 2 - REFLECTION

Deliberately take time to be quiet and to ponder over the most meaningful and powerful experiences you have had and what they mean. Identify the lessons you have learned, and decipher the clues you have uncovered.

Sadly enough, some people are too busy doing good things they never take time to discover the dream that will enable them to do great things. Are you one of those people? When was the last time you allowed yourself peace and quiet where you could ponder with nothing but you and the expanse of the universe?

In the hustle and bustle of life, with a million voices calling you in different directions, it is imperative that you force into your life time where you can deliberately reflect on the lessons your exploration has taught you. Get still, with no distractions, and ask yourself powerful questions. Listen to the answers you receive. It may sound simple, but it is absolutely critical. In the quest for your dream, the only person who can decide whether something is part of your dream, is you! Only consulting other people and outside experiences without taking time to think for yourself is counterproductive.

As I was paying the price for my dream, I routinely took moments to be alone in nature and in other holy places where I could ponder and receive further inspiration. Sometimes I took this time weekly, often I took it daily. I am proud to say that I've filled up multiple notebooks with notes and thoughts related to my dream over the last three years!

As you reflect, avoid the temptation to be discouraged if you don't get big answers right away. The purpose of reflecting is to put puzzle pieces together regarding your dream, and also to discover lessons about who you are and what really matters to you. A dream is a perfect expression of the true you. If you take time to remember who you are, finding your dream will be significantly easier for you than the alternative.

It takes effort to be still, but if your life feels like a bag of responsibilities, tasks, and demands dumped into a blender on the "juice" setting, then reflecting is the phase for you. You've moved enough, and now you get to decide where you actually want to be.

PHASE 3 - IMMEDIATE ACTION

Do not wait for the perfect opportunity – create it. The moment you receive any amount of direction to do something that you feel right about, take immediate action on it. The larger your certainty, the greater action you should take.

This is by far the most underrated piece of advice that dreamers receive from wise mentors. You can philosophize yourself into oblivion, but your understanding of the path before you will ALWAYS be limited to your willingness to progress along it. If your adventuring turns up some promising leads, you've got to make a choice to switch into detective mode. If your busy life doesn't allow for you to have peace and quiet, but you know that you need some deep reflection time, don't wait for everything to settle down in a month – grab your sleeping bag, tell your friends you can't hang with them tonight, and go ponder under the stars.

Now, taking action on the previous two phases is just the start. The real power from this phase happens when you discover a need in the world, a passion that you have, or an aptitude that you feel like you should develop. When you get to that place, this phase means that you build a plan for yourself, and get moving on it immediately.

If you've been talking about becoming a YouTube star, then grab your buddy, borrow a camera, and start shooting.

If you need to overcome a weakness in your life, then get a mentor, sign up for a class, and find a friend to keep you accountable to your goals.

If you have discovered a passion for creative writing, then sign up for NaNoWriMo.

If the poverty of others touches your heart, flex your leadership muscles and create an organization dedicated to gathering donations, teaching people self-reliance, or changing economic policy.

If you're a mathematical genius, spend a month trying to solving a currently debated math problem in the academic world.

The vast majority of my progress towards my dream came because I would get inspired by a new possibility, learn a lesson, and then set up a project for myself to take action on it. Some of my projects have burned and died, but all of them have taught me lessons. I simply can't imagine anyone discovering (let alone actually achieving) their dream without a willingness to DO STUFF.

It is often difficult to understand the joy of something that you've never done before. In some situations, you simply need to do the work in order to experience the result and know if it's what you want. As you take action, you will speedily realize what works and what doesn't. Project by project, you will learn and grow closer to what it is that you must do.

Immediate action is the next step for you if you've had a list of great ideas that you would "love to do someday" working around in your head. There is no better time than now to take act like the hero you were born to be. In the words of one of my favorite mentors, "When would *now* be a good time to take action on your ideas?"

YOU DON'T HAVE TO HAVE IT ALL...YET

Think back to your notes on the Big Dream Formula. Do you have holes? Are things missing? Do you have a purpose statement for your life, but not exactly a big dream? I have two stories from dreamers just like you who were led to discover their dream by starting with one dominant part of the Big Dream Formula, and paying the price from there. These stories will show you two things:

You have a dream

You're closer to it than you realize

The first story is about a young man with a dream that will likely make you laugh at some point in your life. Enter: mastermind artist Joe. Age: eighteen. Super power: drawing advanced stick figures.

Joe came to one of our Lionheart events in the summer of 2016. Quiana and I were on stage together at one point, talking about how to create strategies to overcome obstacles that stand in the way of your dream. When we asked for a volunteer, Joe raised his hand. We brought Joe on stage and talked with him about his dream. He kinda blew us away, and I went on a rant about how he should find a way to have lunch with Stan Lee.

Get this – Joe's dream is to "Create a comic book empire." Does it get any cooler than that? No, no it does not. He already on his way to such an empire, with the publication of his first comic book, The Wizard's Gate. Check it out on Amazon.

Months later, when I asked Joe to write me about his dream, he said this about the event that day: "It was very motivational for me to be able to open up to the group about my passions and goals for the future."

Joe has always loved drawing; it's part of who he is. In his words, "I always knew that I loved drawing comic books, but I didn't really think it was going somewhere until people kept saying, 'You should publish these!' As for finding my dream? I wouldn't really say I felt any different after I found it, it was more of a 'that would be cool' moment.

"I drew comics a lot when I was younger," Joe continues, "With my older brother. I didn't really do much on the 'road to discovery' but I have done a lot after that point. I spent A LOT of time drawing. Once I felt that my art-style was acceptable, I published a book in hopes that people will buy...you can bet that I will be publishing more in the future!"

Joe's advice to all the heroes of the world who haven't found their dream yet is this: "Find something that you really enjoy doing and try sharing it with other people. If they like it, go with the dream. If they don't like it, make sure you actually like it. If you find that you do really enjoy that something, then improve and share with others again."

The second story comes from my own cousin, Abi. Recently married and graduated with her first degree, she's on fire about changing the world and is actively working towards becoming a pediatric oncologist (in english, that's a physician who treats children and adolescents who have been diagnosed with cancer or blood disorders).

Abi discovered her dream through a situation that none of us can envy: when she was nine years old, her younger brother unexpectedly fell sick. When her family investigated, they discovered that he had a tumor in his brain. They fought a long, painful battle to save his life (and they were successful; he's a studmuffin).

"I was in hospitals all the time...and I realized how much I loved the feeling of helping people," Abi wrote, "I loved how heroic his doctors were to him and my parents, but also science and our bodies were so cool to me. So pretty much since then I've dedicated everything I do towards becoming a doctor. It's kind of hard to explain, but I just feel most rewarded when I'm successful, and I love patients and people coming together in trying situations."

An important fact about Abi's story, is that she didn't decide that she wanted to become a pediatric oncologist at nine years old, at the exact moment when her brother was diagnosed with cancer. At that point, she probably hadn't a clue what a pediatric oncologist was! She first paid the price for her dream by enduring with her family the circumstances of cancer recovery. It was *through* that experience that she discovered that she wanted to become a doctor. Abi also paid the price for clarity on what she wanted to do with her life by shadowing doctors and surgeons throughout the following years. By doing so, she realized that surgeons didn't get as much time with their patients as she wanted to have someday, and that led her to explore her other options and find something that suited her even better.

If we choose to let them, our greatest trials can refine us and reveal to us truths about our dream. Sometimes hitting a personal low point can be just what we need to wake up to a big need we are called to set right in the world.

In the fury of hero hype, some people are tempted to believe that the need the grand need they are called to solve exists only far away in a distant land. For a some people, that may be true. But I firmly believe that you've also been placed exactly where you are in life for a reason. Your dream may take you across the world, but you likely don't have to travel across the world to discover it. More often than not, the needs we are closest to are the very ones we are perfectly able to fill.

Joe and Abi found their dreams by starting with an aptitude, passion, or need that was already present in their life. Then they paid the price. Joe paid it through countless hours of action – drawing because he thought it was fun, before he even knew that it was a core part of his dream. Abi paid the price for her dream by staying strong through a harrowing trial that connected her with a big need, and by later actively exploring the field she wanted to serve in.

If there is one thing you take from this chapter, let it be this: there will come a day in your life when you stand before a grand vision of possibility and purpose, and see your dream revealed before you. But you've got to put in the work to get to that place. You will not find the fullness of your dream, except by doing.

Pull out your Dream Journal – what is the #1 thing you need to do right now to move you closer to your dream?

If you don't come up with suitable answers from asking yourself that question, make a plan to apply the Dream Growth Cycle to your I-must-find-my-dream quest. List out what you know, and then based on the phase that you need, decide on specific actions you can take to pay the price for your dream.

If your phase is Exploring, consider making a thirty-day goal to experience new things, or to learn more about one subject.

If your phase is Reflecting, examine the benefits of spending one hour, twice a week, writing and thinking about your dream without any distractions.

If your phase is Immediate Action, I highly suggest designing a project with the purpose of doing good for others. Think of it as a mini dream. Create something that no one is asking you to do, but that is completely from your own initiative and in alignment with what you know about your dream.

As we've discussed in this chapter, the process of refining and growing your dream will require from you a great deal of effort. Some people hesitate at this notion, and avoid ever truly discovering their dream. They don't want to pay the price because they think the price is too high.

The truth is quite the opposite: there are few prices you would rather pay! The effort and time required to discover your dream is anything but drudgery. You're living your dream one dedicated step at a time! You're climbing the mountain of your dream, hunting down the prize that sets the greatest heroes of our world apart from everyone else. Paying the price is nothing short of 100% worth it. With the right attitude, it's even a party.

What's more is that after you've paid the price you'll be inclined to look back over your impressive journey and say, "Wow, did I really do all that?" The result of paying the price for your dream is always a prepared hero, with a heap of collateral accomplishments that happened along the way.

When you are a perfect dreamer, your perfect dream will appear. Until then, pack your bags. You've got a mission to live, and it will be everything you have ever hoped for and more!

Are you willing to pay the price for your dream?

That's what I thought.

Now, go and do.

The 7 Steps to Discovering Your Dream:

1. CHOOSE TO SEEK YOUR DREAM

If you want to find your dream, you need to deliberately search for it. Make the intentional choice to become a dreamer. Naysayers will call this process risky, but the greatest risk is never living at your highest potential. Decide that the answer to what YOU want to do with your life will be found by discovering your dream.

2. KNOW WHAT YOU'RE LOOKING FOR

The more clearly you can define what you want, the more direct your path to obtaining it will be. Study the principles and formulas that characterize dreams. Write out your life purpose. Reflect on your passions, aptitudes, and the needs of the world. Take the time to decide how you'll know YOUR dream when you find it.

3. FREE THE HERO WITHIN

You can't find your dream until you have taken responsibility for your life. It takes a hero to live a dream. Choose to learn of, and believe in, your divine worth and potential. Stop holding yourself back. Instead, give yourself permission to be great.

4. PAY THE PRICE FOR YOUR DREAM

Discovering your dream is as much a journey as achieving it. Sometimes, all you can see is one small step ahead. Get clear about what that next step is, and take it. It will move you in the direction of further clarity. The best way to ensure that you don't figure out what your dream is, is to sit around and wait for it to show up.

Five

THE DREAM GETS BIGGER

There are only two kinds of people in the end: those who say to God, "Thy will be done," and those to whom God says, in the end, "Thy will be done."
~ C.S. Lewis

Well done, Dreamer.

You've made it! No, not just halfway through this book; there's that too, but I'm talking about *your dream*.

Thus far you've learned the first four steps to discovering your dream and figuring out what the heck to do with your life. By reading and applying up to this point, you have done something that most of the world never will: you've chosen your dream.

Congratulations!

You now know the power that a dream has in your life and you've set out to find yours. You are equipped with the vital, unique knowledge of what a dream is. If you believe in your glorious potential, never settling for what is beneath you, and diligently take the steps before you to act upon the knowledge you have while seeking to discover what you still lack, you will inevitably figure out what the heck you want to do with your life.

Not only that, but *you will find your dream!* In fact, if you've honestly taken the steps laid out over the last four chapters, I'm willing to bet that you have already discovered part of it!

Does it feel powerful? Does it inspire you? Does it give you the direction you need in this moment? Does it appear as sweet as you hoped, and yet awesomely incomplete at the same time?

Haha, I know it does. It's part of a dream! *Your dream*.

By taking the first four steps to discovering your dream, you are already beginning to see the fruits of your labor! The more you apply the principles discussed thus far in this book, the more clarity you will receive until a moment comes when someone asks you what you're doing with your life, and you can't help but blurt out a description of your dream, the "why" behind it, and some activities that are moving you forward.

That day will come sooner than you may realize, because you're already on the path towards your dream – and so I say, congratulations! You done good, bruh.

"Woah, woah, woah! Hold up a minute," you may be thinking. "What about the rest of the seven steps to discovering your dream? I've still got a long way to go!"

Chill it, amigo, I've got you covered.

I've used examples of many dreams throughout this book, from youth and young adults at many different mile markers along the path of dream discovery. One said that she wants to become an architect. Another said that she wants to help people find their worth. A third said that his dream is to lead the human race to a higher level of freedom through fitness.

Some of my examples may seem to fit the full definition of a dream more completely than others. Yet regardless of their specificity, I've referred to them all as dreams. Why? Because that's what they are. The same is true of your dream: no matter how vague or concrete, large or small, incomplete or perfect, if you have something that feels to you like a dream should, then you've found your dream!

Yes, there are three more life-changing steps that we haven't talked about yet. But before we get to them, it's important that you understand this truth: You already have the principles and knowledge you need to find all the missing pieces to your dream. In fact, you won't be ready to fully benefit from the fifth step until you have done so. You need what I call, a **Mature Dream** in order to take step number five. You'll know why this is in just a minute.

You likely came to this book because you wanted help figuring out what to do with your life. To me, that answer is very simple: find and live your dream. From there the question becomes, "How do I discover my dream?"

If you understand the principles and actions laid out in the first four chapters of this book, then you already have the answer to this question. Apply those principles and actions to your life, and you will inevitably dig up the clarity and further information that you lack. Next thing we know, you'll be writing me a letter, passionately describing to me how awesome your dream is! (To which I will respond and join in your delightful celebrations).

What I invite you to consider right now, is that the **Awakening Dream** that you've found *is* your dream. It gives you much of the same passion, direction, success, and fulfilment that a fully complete dream will give you.

By saying that you have found your dream, I'm not saying that you have to have a full and complete vision of your dream all written out just yet. A perfect level of clarity doesn't come until you've already achieved your dream and are looking back on it. What is important for you to realize is that no matter how far you've come, if you've made any major breakthroughs regarding your next mission, then you're dealing with a dream that you've discovered. And THAT is beyond being worthy of celebration!

You came to this book looking for your dream. More clarity will always continue to come, but for all practical intents and purposes, you know where you need to take your life. You've found your dream!

The best part?

There's more. Much more.

The next phase of our journey together will be focused less on helping you find a direction to head in and a quest to adventure towards, and more on enabling you to take the concrete mission that you already have to the next level of epicness. This next step is not about finding your dream, but about growing and expanding it.

THE FOUR PHASES OF DREAM DISCOVERY

The fifth step to discovering your dream and knowing for certain what you are called to do with your life can create one of the single most transformational moments of your life so far. But it's the fifth step for a critical reason: it has to be preceded by the other four steps so far laid out in this book. If you haven't sufficiently taken these steps, the fifth step probably won't blow your mind.

So how do you know when you're ready to move on? Short answer: you're ready when step five works for you. Equally useful answer: you're ready when you've uncovered a Mature Dream and are well on your way to accomplishing it.

Said Mature Dream comes as a result of applying the first four steps, and that's one of the reasons why we just congratulated you on your progress. As you'll see, the first four steps are everything you need to obtain a Mature Dream, and therefore be ready for the next level.

Let me break it down for you:

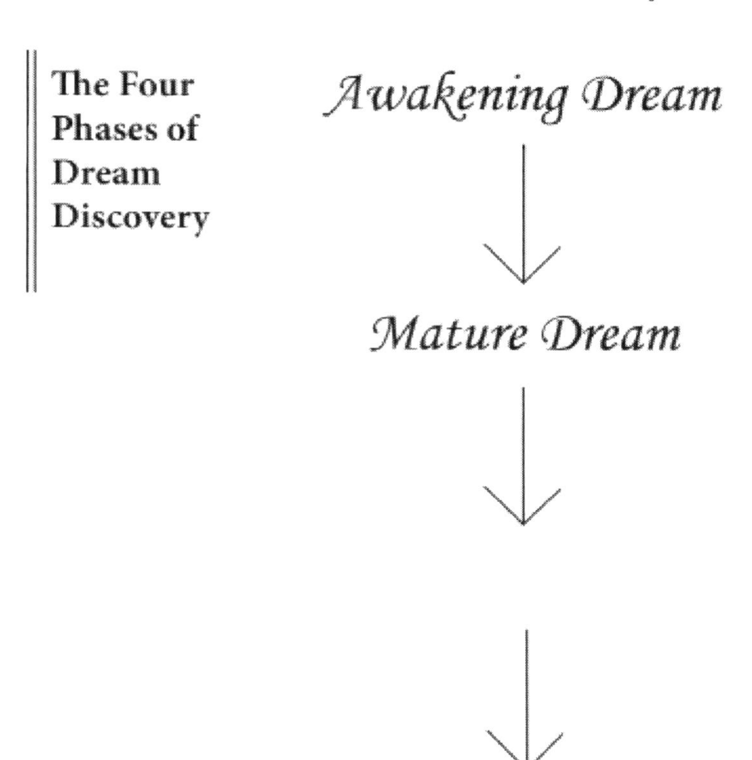

Take a look at the above diagram. It took me an exceedingly long time to create it, what with those mind-bogglingly complex arrows and all.

All dreams begin somewhere in the first phase of dream development, and are, what I call, an Awakening Dream. An Awakening Dream is the level of dream we are talking about when someone realizes that they want to be a dancer. Or that they really love inspiring people. Or when they find a purpose for their life. Or even when they decide that they want to become an internationally renowned speaker and author who also builds businesses that enact social change.

When you get that first breathtaking glimpse of your dream, you're looking at an Awakening Dream. Likewise, when you have a solid semblance of your dream, but you're still missing pieces, you still have an Awakening Dream. This is pretty obvious because, by definition, if you're still waking up to new parts of your dream, one would say that you're in an "awakening" phase.

Your dream begins in this first phase, and as you apply the steps to discovering your dream (especially step number four), you gather missing pieces and refine and test your vision. This process enables your dream to grow and develop. It *matures.*

Once you've paid the price necessary to hone your Awakening Dream, it graduates to the level of a Mature Dream. A Mature Dream is a mission to do something specific to fill a need in the world by using your gifts and passions. It fully fits the official definition of a dream that I laid out in the second chapter. A Mature Dream is complete enough that you know your next steps and big objectives, and you believe that you're perfectly cut out for the tasks ahead. It inspires you and motivates you big time. It naturally compels you to move towards it, and even offers success for your efforts! An unshakable certainty that you know what your dream is, manifested by ambitions actions taken to create it, is great way to know if your dream is a Mature Dream.

DOING VS BECOMING

One of the most telling differences that distinguishes an Awakening Dream from a Mature Dream, is whether it's focus is on *becoming* someone or on *doing* something. Many dreams start out with the desire to become something such as an engineer, a musician, a parent, an athlete, or a million other things – mine certainly did.

My first real glimpse of my dream said that I wanted to become an entrepreneur and thought leader. This occupational angle of viewing your dream in terms of what you will become is a great start, and most people naturally do so. Which makes sense, because in our culture we like to think of careers as the answer to wondering what we should do with our lives. A career-focused description of a dream can be a POWERFUL beginning. It's also a telling indicator of a dream that is still awakening.

Other people start out just knowing that they love an activity, such as working with people, using stories to teach principles, or playing in the adrenaline-pumping arena of extreme sports. Some dreamers begin with the idea that they want to fill a need in the world and help a certain group of people, even though they have no idea how they want to use their gifts and talents to do so; they seek to find a place where they can become someone who gets serve in those ways.

Do you want to become someone who gets to do what you love? Of course! We all do When someone has a dream that's best summed up by a 'becoming' description, they have an Awakening Dream. It's awesome, but still has room to mature. Once they have developed into a skilled and powerful hero who *can* do what they love (or at least has the confidence to), they will then be prepared for a mission to do what they love in a very specific way. That's when their dream becomes mature.

A great example of the difference between the first two phases of dream development is seen in how my personal dream changed after I finished paying the price. At first, my dream was to become a speaker, writer and entrepreneur. Once that dream matured, it became a dream to create a culture of excellence among youth. See the difference?

No matter how it starts out in the Awakening Dream phase, a Mature Dream is fundamentally more about doing than it is about becoming, because doing is the greatest catalyst for you to become the hero that you were born to be and positively impact others. It is through having a destination that you profit by your journey; otherwise you're wandering.

A Mature Dream is a mission for you to achieve, not a person for you to become. Your dream will lead you **to become** something better **by doing** something bigger. As long as your dream is primarily focused on your becoming someone that you want or need to be, but who you have not become yet, it is incomplete – awesome, but incomplete.

If you think your dream might still be an Awakening Dream, that's okay! It can take people anywhere from months to years to work their way to a Mature Dream, because a dream in it's beginning stages will pull you along a process of growing and improving yourself as it develops, and personal growth and change can take time.

If your dream isn't mature yet, you should continue to run down the path ahead of you with reckless abandon. Keep paying the price, and trust the knowledge of your dream that you already have to be a sufficient guide for where you're at in your life.

Before we go on, I need to make something clear: if you're tempted to feel like your dream is second-class because it isn't fully mature yet, then choose not to. I've been sharing stories of many dreams up to this point, on all different levels of maturity, for a reason. Because finding your dream is a journey, not a one-time event, it doesn't much matter where you currently stand on the road to clarity: your dream will serve you no matter where you are. A dream is a dream, no matter how much potential it hasn't realized yet.

So once again, I congratulate you for getting this far! You've already joined the elite club of world-changing-dream-leaders. And if you've actively participated in that club for long enough and have a mature dream in your cherished possession, if your work has paid off and you're already going places, I have a secret for you: It gets even better.

LIGHTHOUSE IN THE NIGHT

If you're anything like me, I bet I can paint a familiar picture for you. It's the picture of what your life looks like when you're diligently building a mature dream. When you're primed to take your dream to the next level, your world will likely look something like this:

You have a dream, and you know that dream is going to change lives *big time*. You've made sacrifices to transition your life towards working on your dream, and that hasn't been easy. You're hustling to make your crazy schedule work, and pull off your ambitious goals. Paying the price has taught you to commit diligently to your dream, and you know how to work hard and get stuff done. You've left the safety of your ordinary life, and are hiking up the mountain that you're at least 95% sure is your dream.

Some people think you're insane, but a lot of them actually look up to you for your accomplishments – especially when they see how much you have on your plate. They congratulate you for "having your life together." You're even starting to see favorable results!

Things are happening. You are going places. Life is good. Busy and sometimes stressful, but good. You are clearly seeing that the direction, motivation and fun that comes from living a Mature Dream is straight up life changing!

Finally, you know what you're supposed to do with your life.

Does that situation sound familiar? Perfect.

It all gets even better when you move on to the next phase of dream discovery, and find your **Big Dream**.

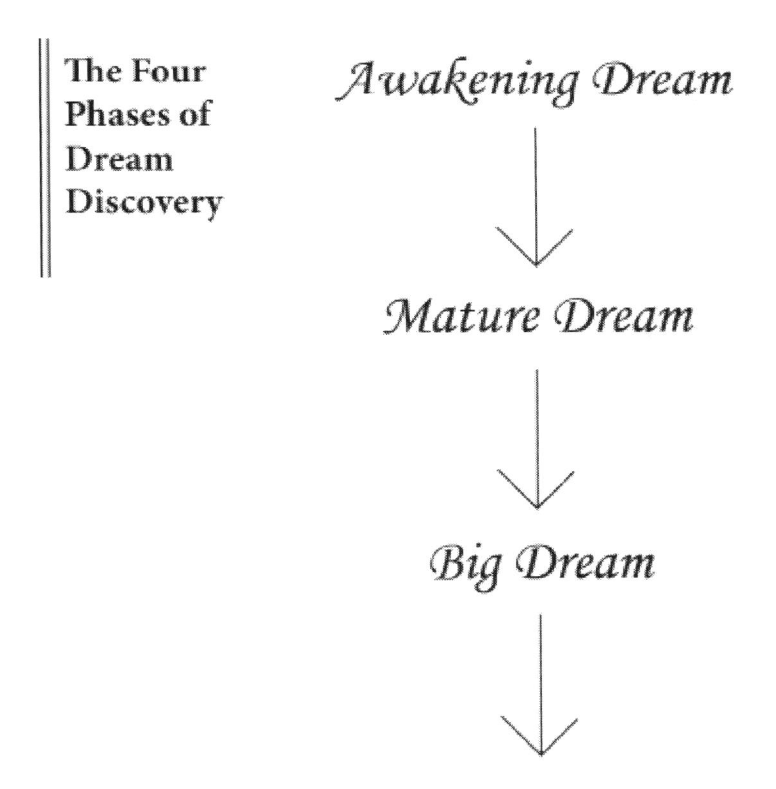

The tricky part to finding a Big Dream, and the reason that not everyone graduates to that level, is that although your Mature Dream still has room to grow, you may not naturally realize there is another level until *after* you find your Big Dream. When you have a Mature Dream, the sense that "something big is missing" isn't overpowering like it is when you have no idea what you want to do with your life – even though something big *is* still missing. That's why Big Dreams often come in moments that we aren't at all expecting.

When you draw closer to the moment when you receive your Big Dream, you may begin to feel uneasy or stressed, but those feelings will likely be mixed up in the natural stress that comes from hustling towards your goals.

"After all," you might think, "I slaved away for a long time to get this dream. I already know what I need to."

If you feel this way, consider this as an opportunity for you to trust that there is something better for you, even if you already have your life together and are doing awesome things. There's a certain amount of pride that comes from slaving away at a noble cause. We need grit and unwavering persistence to achieve our dreams, but every once in awhile we need to take our blinders off and take a look around. If we think that we already have everything figured out all the time, we risk blinding ourselves to seeing a *bigger* picture of the mission we say we care so much about.

You've got to trust that your Big Dream will be better than your Mature Dream. This trust is absolutely critical. Thankfully, you only have to trust for a relatively short moment. Once you discover your Big Dream, your life changes in such a way that a part of you will wonder how you ever survived without it. Unlike a Mature Dream, a Big Dream doesn't show up piece by piece over an extended period of time. Rather, it is revealed in a small handful of (or even just one) brilliant moments.

The moment in which you first discover your Big Dream will feel a lot like how the crew of a ship might feel when they suddenly see the beacon of a lighthouse illuminating their path. This "lighthouse moment" is the best way I know to describe what it's like to behold your Big Dream.

Imagine that you are the captain of a ship that has been sailing through the ocean all night. You are approaching your destination just as the darkest hours of the morning fall upon you. Between you and the safe harbor lies a coast filled with reefs and rocks that will tear your vessel to shreds, should you run aground. You have labored diligently to get to land, using the stars to navigate.

As you plot your next move, you rely on the light of the stars and what's left of the moon to strategically pick out a safe approach to the harbor. The problem is, you're in completely unfamiliar waters. You don't even know if all the rocks are visible from the surface of the water!

Eventually, you think you have it figured out – well enough, anyways. Your hard work has produced a solid plan. It's not perfect, and it looks like it might be near impossible to pull off, but you *have to make it work*. Your life and the lives of other people are relying on you to bring them to safety! You can't back away from the daring mission before you.

"I can do this," you say, as you grit your teeth against the odds.

A brilliant light suddenly explodes above the harbor. The beacon of a lighthouse has been lit! Compared to this light, the stars and moon are completely overpowered. The light pours out onto the waters before you, directing you along a new path to your destination.

You could technically still follow your carefully laid plan, but with the new revelation, who would resist making whatever changes necessary to follow the light? You thought you knew before, and that knowledge was sufficient for you to get this far. But now you know beyond a shadow of a doubt!

With the lighthouse shining from the coast, you find yourself beholding the magnificent promise of land beyond the coast. With perfect clarity on the path before you, you are able to focus your attention on what *else* is possible for your dream. Even as you set aside elements of what you thought you had to do, room is made for something bigger – something more perfectly you.

The light that shines upon you is warm, brilliant, and filled with possibility. You know exactly where you need to be. You still don't see every single step before you, but you don't need to. Your path feels almost as clear as day!

If you can imagine such a beautiful moment, then you have a good idea what it feels like to behold your Big Dream. Though this moment is not one that will happen frequently in the journey to your dream, it is a blessedly critical one.

A Big Dream is defined, more than anything else, by the feeling of a "lighthouse moment." It's a tipping point where your Mature Dream gets shifted into a place that enables you to see the mission ahead of you with so much clarity that you can't imagine doing anything else. It's an overwhelming moment where your perspective is expanded. Your dream still fits the official definition of a dream, but it does so on a massively new level that makes your previous ambitions feel adorably inadequate.

A Big Dream still isn't complete, of course, but that's to be expected. Your dream can't be complete until it has been completed; it can't be complete until after you've achieved it, and are looking back over the path you have trod. This final perspective is known as the fourth phase of dream discovery. When your Big Dream has been sufficiently fulfilled, it becomes a Complete Dream.

Behold, la diagram:

The Four Phases of Dream Discovery

Awakening Dream

↓

Mature Dream

↓

Big Dream

↓

Complete Dream

Notice how you'll never get to a Complete Dream without a Big Dream? There's a profound piece of wisdom in this: if you never take the fifth step to discovering your dream, you will ever chase your dream and never be able to fully achieve it. No matter what you do, the most perfect completion of it can never be reached.

Some people never take this next step, and they consequently never discover their Big Dream. They find great success, and they go places! A pre-Big-Dream is great place to be, and I don't mean to undervalue the joy of a dream at the Mature level. In fact, most of the people who "follow their dreams" achieve all their success without a Big Dream.

Such heroes do great things – and they also miss out on something even greater. They miss out on a more perfect expression of who they are. They live adventures, but they miss out on the greatest of all adventures. They never quite have their "lighthouse moment".

The reason we've laid out the boundaries between the phases of dream development, is because the fifth step of dream discovery plays a sequentially critical role in the life of a dreamer. The first four steps are designed to get you to the point of a Mature Dream. The fifth step provides maximum benefit only after you're ready for it, so you have to understand the different places you can be.

Without a Mature Dream, the following information will be interesting for you to ponder in theory, but it can't transform you. You've got to have a dream before you can improve it.

We good? Excellent.

It's time for your dream to graduate to a much BIGGER level.

MY DIVINE QUEST

I am about to share a story that changed my life forever. It is a story that I hold close to my heart. This story is of a precious moment in which my dream radically shifted and became a Big Dream. It's the story of how I let go of the dream I had slaved away at for months, only to find it again on a whole new level.

Within a few days following Quiana's text about doing public speaking for youth, I made some big sacrifices towards living the mission I felt called to. For weeks I had been feeling a deep desire to focus even more heavily on the projects with my blog, and along with that, this new thing called Lionheart Mentoring. I felt that this was the next step for me, and with that clarity, I took fast steps towards living it:

I quit my job at a local smoothie shop (even though I was the self-proclaimed Smoothie King and could make a to-die-for Strawberry Squeezer in less than 90 blendsational seconds), I dropped my credit load in half for the upcoming semester of college, I dove into redesigning the blog that Celine and I ran, and I started speaking with Lionheart where we could. I had opened up extra time in my life, and was doing what I could with what I had before me. I was payin' that price, don't you know.

Throughout the next two months, I hustled like mad. Rather than taking a nice long Christmas break, I slaved away for long hours at the computer and on the phone. I was motivated, I was focused, and I was moving towards my dream. Things were going pretty great, and although I hadn't "made it" yet, I was living my dream!

It wasn't easy or comfortable, and definitely felt like the going-through-the-grind-before-any-measure-of-success part of the dream journey, but every dream requires that phase. I was excited, because I was on a mission to make a specific, and monstrous impact on the culture of my peers.

In retrospect, I realize that it did feel like something special was missing, but I didn't know what to do about it except move forward until new inspiration struck. I was doing my best, trusting that my dream would pan out. I had people to help me and cheer me on, and I trusted that future opportunity would soon show up. I would take action on what I had, more clarity would show up, and I'd take action on that to arrive at more clarity. The cycle of dream growth continued.

Clarity did arrive, just not like I expected.

I was expecting to see as far as the next hill I need to climb. What I actually saw, was the summit of a marvelous mountain. And t wasn't even the same mountain as the one I thought I was on track to reach! Similar, but a different mountain altogether!

I thought I already knew exactly what I wanted, but what I discovered forever altered my dream. It changed my direction, and gave me everything that I had unknowingly been missing.

In hindsight, the dream that I had been fighting for was nothing close to as powerful, peaceful, and life-changingly important as the mission that unveiled before me. The lighthouse illuminated a better way.

My moment came as I was finishing up day three of a self-improvement and leadership seminar. It was the kind of thing that most people find either completely life changing or a little on the weird side. (I think both parties are correct: the weirdness is the price you pay for learning something new.) I was there with Quiana, Dallin, and a few other ambitious friends.

At this moment, I was watching people do trust falls. I was in a massive conference room, with a few hundred adult participants standing in tightly packed groups throughout the floor. Music played distantly. The chairs stood in stacks around the edges. The trust fall activity was designed to help people move past their fear by learning to trust and love, but I wasn't paying much attention.

Instead, I was drifting from group to group, consumed by my own dilemma. I was working so hard to live my dream, but this day I just didn't know if what I was doing was really going to make a difference. I knew I was powerful and capable, but I needed my next step badly.

As I wandered through the packed area, I was awestruck by the personal transformation and newfound freedom I saw occurring in the lives of strangers. I sensed that this experience was connected with my dream somehow. The question I wanted an answer to, was "How?"

How can this experience teach me about my dream?

How can I inspire and change people?

How can I achieve the next step to my goals?

How can I be, truly be, who I was born to be?

Just...How?

I felt a burning need to know, but my utter lack of understanding left me deeply humbled.

In this moment of confusion, I decided that I wasn't going to worry about deciphering and strategizing this one out. I needed insight beyond what I already knew. I needed to solve a puzzle that I didn't have all the pieces to. So right then and there, as I slowly meandered under artistic chandeliers, I submitted to a power far greater than myself.

My silent prayer was simple: "God, what do you want me to do?"

This wasn't the first time I prayed like this. Historically speaking, an answer always came, but this time my preparation and timing prepared the way for a big reveal.

"I will do whatever you tell me," I said. "Please show me the way."

The answer came simple and direct:

"Do you see the freedom these people are experiencing?"

Of course I did. The atmosphere was electric and full of divine possibility; it was entirely different from the underwhelming rituals of everyday, normal person life.

I thought about the millions of youth across the world. I thought of the many who were held captive by a misunderstanding of who they were and of their full potential, limited by a lack of knowledge regarding the principles of virtue and freedom, and trapped by doubt and fear. I thought also of the thousands of magnificent leaders in our rising generation who were itching for a chance to do great good.

"Bring this feeling of empowerment, love, and connection to the youth of the world," the answer continued. "Be my hands; lift them up when I cannot." These words filled my soul with a burning feeling of peace.

To you, this experience may not seem to have produced a very straightforward game plan. But in that moment, the message was perfect for me. After all I had learned and worked for and experienced as I had paid the price over and over for my dream, I knew what it meant. I saw the glorious peak of my dream in the distance, and that view was everything I needed.

I knew that I was being given a shot to do something over the next year and a half that had never been done before! It was big, it was intimidating, it was audacious; it would allow me to spend hundreds of hours doing things I love to do, and at the same time, also require me to use my greatest skills and natural gifts – the things people have been telling me I was a natural at all my life: I could speak, write, gather people, build systems, organize teams, and decipher principles that would enable us to build a movement that would someday impact millions!

Most importantly, I was being given an opportunity to lead the already powerful youth in the world in rising to their best selves, and thereby join with me in serving and blessing the world in a greater way than we ever could on our own. Together, we would work miracles! At last, the young heroes of the world would not have to wonder if they could do great things; they would know it! I could solve the need that I cared so much about, and in a way that exceeded the potential depth and reach of any of my previous plans.

I sat on the floor against the deserted wall of the conference room amid stacks of chairs, and cried as I wrote in my Dream Journal. The tears of peace, joy, and gratitude for the overwhelming perfection of my Big Dream gently threatened the pages as I scribbled down my inspiration. The event would soon end, and I would return to my work with Lionheart, this time with a glimpse of the magnitude of what we were actually supposed to do.

I didn't know every exact step I needed to take, but at the same time, I knew exactly what I needed to do. This Big Dream was a mission and a calling that I was willing to sacrifice almost everything to achieve. My life, and the lives of countless heroes would never be the same.

I've thought a lot about the day of my landmark lighthouse moment. My study and pondering has led me to discover the action required by that sacred experience in which a dream ceases to be simply "my dream," and becomes a Big Dream. This action is encompassed in the fifth step to finding your dream and understanding your present mission: **Submit Your Dream To Something Greater**.

Submitting your dream to something greater means listening, with complete humility and intent to take action, to a greater source of wisdom and power for instruction about what your dream is. Among other things, this requires that you be ready to change your direction if the answer requires it. It means that you have to put everything about your dream up on the negotiation table, ready to walk away from all of it if that's your next step. Only when you do this, can you truly listen; only when you submit your hard-earned "musts" can you make room for something greater.

When you submit your dream to something greater, you choose to look away from the starry sky and your navigational maps and trust not only that a lighthouse will appear when the time is ripe, but that it is a guide worthy of your greatest dreams, hopes and desires.

To submit you must believe that a force greater than yourself can and will guide you to heights and that you could never reach on your own; through complexities that would take many lifetimes to experiment on. To listen like you need to for your dream to enter this next phase of it's discovery, you must be willing to surrender the focus of your ambition, your expectations and plans, and even your need to have a dream in the first place.

Without this moment of submission, you could continue to change the lives of others, do what you're passionate about, and utilize your personal aptitudes – the basic definition of a dream. But in the midst of all the success you thought you wanted, you'll someday realize that something big is missing. You'll realize that you don't feel on fire about your life and you don't have the light in your eyes that characterizes passionate dreamers. You'll begin to wonder what purpose your life has, and perhaps even wonder what you should do with your life. Back to square one you would go.

The fifth step is a refining moment for you and your dream. You must submit to something greater because if you do not, your dream will be banished from it's highest path of growth. Big Dreams don't come from you, they come from a greater source. If your dream was about only you and from only you, its size and power would be limited to only you.

A Big Dream is far, far greater than any one person. Far more influential, too. Ask any dreamer who has submitted to something greater, and they will tell you that when they chose to submit their dream, they became more powerful than their past self had ever imagined. Like when Obi-Wan submitted his life to the Force in the fourth Star Wars movie, but for real and not preceded by an underwhelming lightsaber fight with Darth Vader.

WHERE DOES YOUR LIGHT COME FROM?

I have pondered long and hard about whether there was another way to go about finding your Big Dream other than submitting to something greater. There simply is not. If you want a dream that is greater than yourself, and more needed and more influential than you can contrive on your own, then you *must* trust a greater source of guidance!

The question is, what greater thing will you choose to submit to?

We might differ on the larger-than-us thing that we give our dream to, but if you don't already know what you need to submit to, then ask yourself this question: "What force, power, cause, or being is the greatest that I know?"

Because why would you submit your dream, and yourself, to a power that was less than the greatest and highest source of purpose, wisdom, and light?

I have asked this question myself many a time; I know what my answer is, and what force I submit to. In writing this book, another cause of my long ponderings and internal debates was whether it mattered specifically what or who you submit to. I believe that it does, and that the source that you choose to submit to will influence the Big Dream that you receive – some for better, others for worse.

You must be the one to make the choice to submit, and you must decide what truth is worthy of your submission. I'm not here to tell you how to make that choice. What I am here to do, is to show you the source that I have seen, time and time again, from every dreamer I have ever learned of or witnessed discover a Big Dream, be the only perfect source of power and guidance.

If my experience, reasoning, and observations prove any merit, the most effective force to submit to, by a landslide, is God.

By using the term "God," we need to be clear about something. I'm not talking about submitting to the "universe." Not to a mystical "higher power" or "higher good." Not to the cosmic forces of nature. Not to the inner light that connects us as human beings. Not to a theoretical conception of a being that plays no active role in the workings of mankind. While I believe that there is truth to all of those perspectives, they represent something of an Awakening God, if you catch my drift.

I'm talking about *God*. You know, the one you pray to when your world is falling apart (and hopefully when it's falling together, too).

If you want to jump straight to your Big Dream, a guaranteed way is to submit to a divine and perfect being who knows you better than you know yourself. A being who can see what neither you, nor anyone else, can see. A being who delights in enabling the heroes of the world to serve one another and live glorious adventures. Give your hard-earned dream to the God who cares enough about you to give you a greater one in return.

I'm not making a case about how any one religion is better than any other. That's far outside a necessary discussion for your quest to discover your dream. On the contrary, I believe that God speaks to anyone who sincerely desires to know His will for them. And that's enough for you to find your Big Dream.

So go and ask the Creator of all light to shed a ray on your present situation. That's what I do, anyways. Works every time.

Pull out your Dream Journal and write out a summary of your dream. Then, with that summary in mind, answer this question: "What greater source is worthy of me submitting my dream to?"

The act of submitting your dream to something greater is a lot like of making a gift out of your dream. What happens to it after that is dependant on who you give it to and how you give it. If you give it to the wrong source or for the wrong reasons, you won't get a Big Dream in return – you'll probably just end up more confused and frustrated than you ever have been before in your life. If you give your dream as a gift to the right source, you will be given back the gift of a bigger, purer dream.

Whatever force, power, truth, idea, cause, or being you choose to submit to, you'll know that you've submitted it to the right source when you feel peace. That doesn't mean it's going to feel easy. You are sacrificing your hard earned dream after all. But once you've chosen to trust the right power, a feeling of peace will confirm the correctness of your decision. If the initial fright of vulnerability and surrender doesn't convert into a feeling of peace, then you need to reevaluate either how you submitted, or whether you submitted to the right source.

Some people submit their dream to fear, doubt, pleasure, or the expectations of others. Some people submit their dream to a system, or the sole pursuit of money or power. Some people submit their dream to "enlightened philosophies." Those sources are lower than your dream, and should not be submitted to. You should master and rise above such things.

If you give your it to the wrong source – that is, a power, being, cause or idea that is not worthy of your dream – you'll feel empty, restless, and powerless. There's a critical difference between submitting your dream to something greater and giving up it.

Speaking of giving up, with all this talk of submission, that's something we need to be clear on: submitting your dream to something greater DOES NOT MEAN GIVING UP ON IT. Yes, you recognize that you can't find a Big Dream on your own. No, you don't throw up your hands and decide that this is the last straw – the doubts inside of you always said that you didn't have a dream to begin with anyways. No, you don't curl into a moppy ball in a blanket and surrender your power, apathetically laying down before the challenges of the world.

You're a hero, dang it! Your dream is still your joy and responsibility! The point here is that if you submit your powerful nature and vision, you can be shown something greater than you now understand. But that same submission requires that you *be* powerful. A dream can't grow to the next level if you throw it away.

This isn't the part where you care less about your dream; it's the part where you care *more*. Care enough to allow it to grow beyond you. That's where true dedication happens. Care enough to open your dream (and subsequent life plan) to be molded and refined, bringing everything about your dream to the table, so that a greater craftsman can adjust it to fit you better.

Do you understand now why you can't take the fifth step until you already know what your dream is, and how without this step, your dream will be limited? Your passions and aptitudes, as well as your perception of the needs in the world have been critical in getting you this far, but right now you need to forget about what you think you want and trust that the greater power that you submit to can see your dream more clearly than you can.

Ultimately, this requires your choice to submit your *will* to the will of that greater source of wisdom. This principle (indeed, the entire fifth step) may seem counterintuitive, because what you're looking for is *your dream*, after all. Shouldn't it come from you?

Life is full of paradoxes. The paradox I'm showing you here is that in order to find your dream you must work with all your might to discover what you want, and then surrender that hard earned desire, believing that what you really want will stay and what is an illusion will be replaced with something better. Your dream requires your work, but your work alone is not enough.

It is not possible to deduce your Big Dream; you must listen for it.

It is also not possible to hear your dream without first deducing it.

A ship does not navigate into existence the guidance of a lighthouse.

A ship also cannot see the lighthouse until it navigates to the harbor.

HOW TO GET A BIG DREAM

Are you willing to undergo a moment of trust, and find your Big Dream?

Let's make this idea practical – well, as practical as we can. I can't spell out for you exactly what your process of submitting your dream to something greater will look like, or how you'll receive your Big Dream, just like I can't tell you what your dream is. The experience will be unique to you.

What I can lay out, is the general process of finding your Big Dream. It looks like this:

1. **Live your dream.** We talked about this, and you already know what it means.

2. **Trust that something greater than yourself can direct you to your Big Dream.** For me, this "something greater" is God: I trust God to be the ultimate source of Big Dreams.

3. **Be humble enough to seek divine guidance.** Humility is the key that enables you to clearly see the world and all of it's

opportunity. Anyone can find a dream; only the humble will live a Big Dream.

4. **Temporarily clear your slate.** Put everything on the table, being completely okay with walking away from any or all of it if you are called to do so. In my story, I said, "I'll do *anything* you want me to do."

5. **Ask about your dream.** *What will you have me do?*

6. **Listen.** Listening means that you don't just hear an answer, but that you let the truth sink into your heart with full intent to take action. The answer will likely come softly, and it will be accompanied by a feeling of peace.

If you get a life-altering, Big-Dream-revealing, let's-throw-illegal-fireworks-into-the-street-due-to-excitement answer, then boom! You've had your lighthouse moment. If you do not, that doesn't mean that the process doesn't work for you or that God doesn't care about you.

The truth is quite the opposite, actually.

One of the most critical facts to note about my personal lighthouse moment was that it had less to do with the seminar I was attending (even though the incredible environment did prime me for clearing my slate and listening), and everything to do with how prepared I was. I had actually attended the same event two months prior, and at that time, walked away having gained clarity, tools, and a heap of inspiration to continue living my dream.

That first time I attended, I was spurred onward towards my Mature Dream. But I didn't get a Big Dream until two months later. I had listened both times. I had been quick to act and pay the price both times. The difference was that the second time, I was ready.

When you are ready, and your moment does come, you'll recognize it. This part of the dream journey is a gift. You don't get to manage your way into a dream that's larger than you are. That's absurd. You get to prepare and relish the victories of living your Mature Dream – which are moving you in the right direction and enabling you to serve others and impact the world in the best way you presently can – until you are called to live a Big Dream. When that day happens, and I trust that it will happen soon for you, your life will never be the same.

If you are currently in the stressful hustle of a Mature Dream and you sense that there might be something bigger that your dream is missing, then I invite you to take your dream journal and find a quiet place. Armed with your preparation, humility, and trust, submit your dream to something greater.

Your sacred moment of clear instruction could be knocking at your door. Bend the knee of the powerful hero that you are. Look up from your plans and expectations. There is a beacon of light pointing the way to a destiny and mission more glorious than you could ever wish for.

Your Big Dream is before you.

What do you see?

The 7 Steps to Discovering Your Dream:

1. CHOOSE TO SEEK YOUR DREAM

If you want to find your dream, you need to deliberately search for it. Make the intentional choice to become a dreamer. Naysayers will call this process risky, but the greatest risk is never living at your highest potential. Decide that the answer to what YOU want to do with your life will be found by discovering your dream.

2. KNOW WHAT YOU'RE LOOKING FOR

The more clearly you can define what you want, the more direct your path to obtaining it will be. Study the principles and formulas that characterize dreams. Write out your life purpose. Reflect on your passions, aptitudes, and the needs of the world. Take the time to decide how you'll know YOUR dream when you find it.

3. FREE THE HERO WITHIN

You can't find your dream until you have taken responsibility for your life. It takes a hero to live a dream. Choose to learn of, and believe in, your divine worth and potential. Stop holding yourself back. Instead, give yourself permission to be great.

4. PAY THE PRICE FOR YOUR DREAM

Discovering your dream is as much a journey as achieving it. Sometimes, all you can see is one small step ahead. Get clear about what that next step is, and take it. It will move you in the direction of further clarity. The best way to ensure that you don't figure out what your dream is, is to sit around and wait for it to show up.

5. SUBMIT YOUR DREAM TO SOMETHING GREATER

Because a Big Dream is greater than you, it must ultimately come from a greater source. After you have paid the price for your dream, you must be willing to give it all up in exchange for something better. Trust the greatest source of light and wisdom you can find. When the time is right, your trust will be answered with a glorious mission for you to fulfil.

Six

HURTLING OFF THE EDGE

Sacrifice is what turns your preparation into service for another human being.
~ Joshua David

"I am scaarrred for Dallin..." my voice quietly trailed off on the camera's audio recording as I angled it to capture the figure of my best friend, and record the monumental occasion. I was perched precariously on the narrow tip of a very pointy outcropping of rock that rose out of the lake, it's base a dozen feet from the shore. It would have been a perilous experience climbing up there – in my barefoot and camera-toting situation – was I not secretly a ninja in my free time. Something like that.

I figured it was okay to live life on the edge every now and then. Especially for the purpose of helping someone make personal history and crush their limits.

I attached the video camera to a well used tripod, held together mainly by duct tape. I left it in a secure position, and hurried down from my vantage point and then back up the neighboring forty foot cliff to where one of my personal heroes, Dallin, stood in resolution. He was about to hurl himself off the cliff into the lake below.

Dallin had never been cliff jumping before. Normally, he even avoided diving boards. Now, he peered over the edge at the water which lay a dizzying distance below. As I watched him mentally prepare himself for the moment ahead, I mentally noted that I have never seen a human being more terrified, yet simultaneously determined, in my entire life. That opinion still stands to this day.

Dallin had a minor-phobia of two things: deep water and heights. He had lived with these fears since childhood, and they had been reinforced by multiple traumatic experiences throughout his life. So naturally, we decided to put him on the top of a cliff and shove him off into a cold lake!

Did I mention that Dallin really doesn't do well in the the cold either?

This was in August of 2015, three months before Lionheart was founded. Dallin was currently slaving away at studying for college admissions tests and I was about to begin school at BYU. The two of us had been recently feeling like this cliff-jumping escapade was an important symbolic experience about pushing through fears that we needed to have. And hey, what else would two teenage boys get up to do at 6:00am on a Saturday morning?

Dallin may have been having regrets about our trip as he stood there at the edge, contemplating his fate, but I at least thought it was a fun morning already! I would later understand that this adventure was a moment that symbolized a far, far more than fun.

I pulled out my phone, and settled into a good filming position a few yards from the drop zone.

"When you jump, make sure to leap far away from the edge," I cautioned. "If you don't, you'll crash into the side on the way down!"

Dallin assured me he wouldn't hesitate. There was a slight shake in his voice. His face was white as a sheet, and not for lack of a tan.

Wow, I thought to myself, *He's really scared. And he's really going to do this.*

I pressed the video button on my phone.

I was recording Dallin's jump because he was making a video to lead out on what we called *The Fear Challenge*, a project we initiated with the blog Celine and I had recruited him and some other youth to help run. The challenge consisted of us doing something we feared and then challenging our friends to do likewise and prove that fear would not master our lives. Cool, right?

Little did I know, there was also a deeper reason that Dallin was facing his monster of fear; one that he would speak of often in the following years.

It was the fight against human sex trafficking.

It is estimated that hundreds of thousands of children are currently being held in slavery around the world, for the sole purpose of being rented for sex. Yes, children, some as young as three years old. It's a horrible evil in our world. A few years back, an Ex-Special Forces veteran by the name of Timothy Ballard dedicated his life to putting an end to this evil. His organization, Operation Underground Railroad (O.U.R.) leads the fight. Maybe you've heard of it.

Dallin had been approached by a mutual friend of ours, Emily, who was on a mission to raise a donation of $50,000 for O.U.R. She was fifteen years old at the time, and Dallin knew that she and her team of friends could use his help. Emily was putting on a fundraiser and needed items for a silent auction to be donated by local businesses. Dallin had set out one afternoon under her direction, to approach local businesses and use the powerful meaning of their cause and his smooth sales skills to get a bunch of items donated. That was his plan, anyways.

He hadn't gotten *anything* donated for the fundraiser that afternoon or any other day, because when it came time to talk to the business owners he had let his doubt of himself and his fear of rejection cause him to chicken out and give only a half-hearted effort.

This bothered him deeply. His fears and doubts had limited him, and as a result he had failed to help people in desperate need of his assistance. Even if his failure didn't change much in the grand scheme of things, the reason for his failure was what really worried him.

As Dallin stood on the edge of this cliff, he told himself that if he could conquer this fear, that is, leap off a (*mostly*) safe cliff and plunge forty feet into a frigid lake below, he knew he would have the courage to do everything in his power to save, protect, and bless the lives of everyone in his life who he was called to serve.

It was time for him to leap.

The water below looked like a floor of smooth, greenish-brown cement. It held mystery, and it wasn't hard to find oneself doubting the promised safety of a soft landing. Dallin slowly made his way to the rocky and uneven edge. I steadied the filming camera.

After a long moment of facing his inner demons – the voices screaming in his head, telling him that he wasn't strong enough, that it was too frightening, and to back down and go home – he turned to face me.

"I am Dallin, and I do not let fear control my actions!"

I held my breath, and he leaned forward, then jumped.

There was silence for two long seconds as he disappeared from my view, hurtling through the air.

I scrambled to the edge following the splash, just in time to see Dallin pop up out of the water. I hurried down and around to the shore to meet him.

When I reached the shore he was giddily splashing around in the shallow water, singing a random song about cows. The good-natured, silly Dallin was back. Every word he spoke rang with victory and the pure enjoyment of being *alive*!

No matter the obstacle, he would choose to stop at nothing to do the work he was called to do; to uplift suffering people in great need. These bonds of fear and doubt chained him no more!

As Dallin spent the next year inspiring and teaching people from the stage, he would often tell the story of him jumping off that cliff. He would do this because his story is a quite literal example of a moment that every dreamer must encounter: a leap of faith.

"Ah yes, the famous leap of faith," you might say to yourself. "That's what you do when you step outside of your comfort zone and do something you're afraid of that results in personal growth. I face those all the time!"

Indeed, you do face fear all the time. And a high caliber dreamer like you is probably used to blasting right through the opposition. It is truly impossible for you to get to the point where you have a Big Dream without braving the unfamiliar many a time.

A leap of faith is the choice to push through a wall of fear and doubt that stands in the way of you being the hero you were born to be and living your dream. A leap of faith is a drastic step outside of what you consider comfortable and what you feel is familiar. It is a moment of facing a necessary risk with the real possibility of failure, and acting on the realization that success at your dream is worth a million failures. A leap could require a drastic commitment of time, resources, energy, or all three at once!

Although all leaps of faith will feel challenging, the outward mechanics of them can be big or small, depending on where you are in your journey. Learning to live by faith is a lesson that a successful life will require you to learn many times over. Whether it's in the pursuit of a dream, or just as you strive to grow yourself as a person, fear and doubt will always be at the edge of your comfort zone. When you push through that fear and doubt in a bold way to get what you want, you take a leap of faith.

For example, if your dream is to be an amazing dancer, but you don't have time to dance at a studio because you're working part time, taking all honors high school classes, and participating in student body leadership roles so that you can be on the fast track to a prestigious school, your leap of faith might be to drop all the things that make you look like a "high achiever," so that you can achieve at something you care about far more. It might also look like throwing away your plans to go to the prestigious college altogether!

Or let's say that you don't know what your dream is exactly yet, but you know that your next step is to explore the world. You have always wanted to visit another country, but you've never even applied for a passport. In that situation, your leap of faith might be to grab a buddy or family member, pool your savings, and book a pair of plane tickets.

And if you dream of being an entrepreneur/chef, and of opening up your own gourmet cafe, but had never gotten past the planning and hoping phase because you you were too busy with your unfulfilling, full-time job, then your leap of faith might be walking into your boss's office and quitting so you can build your dream business.

These leaps of faith are super scary, relatively "irresponsible," and at the same time, absolutely thrilling. Do you feel the excitement of them? Do you feel the audacity and unfettered *possibility* that shape these leaps? Do you feel the *realized dream* within them?

Good, because if you've recently discovered clarity on your dream, then your next leap might be right around the corner. And it's going to be epic.

THE LEAP OF ALL LEAPS

Have you ever noticed that the way planets look and move through space is eerily similar to how their atomic-level friends look and move? Or how the Golden Ratio can be found in ancient Greek architecture as well as in the shape of a seashell you might pick up on the beach? True principles often mirror one another on different levels of scale. The same is true of the steps you must take in order to discover your dream and figure out what the heck you want to do with your life.

Each of the seven steps to discovering your dream can be found on both a micro and a macro level – in the day to day living of your dream, and also in the long-term discovery of it. You can see the steps as one-time phases that sequentially progress from one to another, and at the same time, as actions that a dreamer must live every day of his or her life.

It's like how even though submitting your dream to something greater is something you can and should do on every level of your dream, there is also a special time for your submission that leads to a lighthouse moment. You'll pay the price for any knowledge of your dream, and there is also a specific time in your journey when all you're doing is paying the price. Freeing the hero within is critical at any time that life gets you down, but it's also a foundational place that you need to reach before you can find your dream. As for choosing to dream and knowing what a dream looks like...I think you get the idea.

This same pattern applies to leaps of faith. Living the principle of taking leaps of faith wherever they show up is absolutely necessary for you to live a successful, adventurous, and dream-filled life. You simply can't get by without them – nor would you want to! That said, there does come a moment when a particularly gigantic leap of faith will categorize the next step in discovering your dream.

If you observe enough people who have lived Big Dreams, you will notice that there was, without fail, a day when they had to take a leap of faith that made most other leaps associated with that dream seem little in comparison. They had to take on a risk that felt so massive that it shook them to their core. They were required to do something that compelled the voices in their head (and sometimes those of the people around them) to scream that what they were doing was crazy, ludicrous, insane.

This is a special moment that occurs sometime after a dreamer receives their Big Dream. Because a Big Dream is much greater than yourself, you must begin to live on a much bigger level in order to fulfil it. And that transition isn't a comfortable one. As a general rule of thumb, the bigger the dream, the bigger the leap of faith required.

The leap of faith moment is a thrilling part of every dreamer's journey, but it is also a very real challenge that will undoubtedly test your limits. Nothing that you can't overcome, but a test worthy of the hero that you truly are. You will take many leaps of faith throughout your life, as you live dream after dream and as the dreams expand and compound upon one another to grow in challenge and impact.

So if you've had your lighthouse moment and discovered a very Big Dream, get ready to face your inner demons; your greatest test yet is about to debut. In fact, you might already see a leap of faith directly before you.

Are you facing an obstacle or challenge that looks really, really intimidating, or maybe even terrifies you to the core? Does the next step towards your big dream require you to start something big, or change your life in major ways? Do you know where you need to go, but have no idea where how things are going to work out?

Pause for a moment and ask yourself this: "Is now the time for me to take a leap of faith?"

If you're intuitively feeling a yes, and you have a good idea of what you need to do, write down your answer in your Dream Journal. If you don't know what your leap of faith is, or if you're thinking, "*I don't know Jacob,* do *I need to take a leap of faith right now?"* then take notes and apply the following methods. Also pay attention to the stories you hear about other people taking leaps of faith. While yours won't look exactly the same as theirs does, something about their leap might jump out at you.

One straightforward tool that is useful for recognizing what your next leap is, is using your fear and doubt to guide you to what you need to do. Often times, it's the one thing that we force away deep into our subconscious because we don't *want* to think about it because it's so terrifying or hard, that we truly need to do. When a vision of our leap of faith finally comes to mind, we might be tempted to think up a million other things that we could do instead – smaller cliffs that aren't quite as high.

Our fear and doubt can sometimes blind us to our obvious next step. It's possible that you'll wake up to your leap of faith after weeks of searching, only to realize that you knew what it was all along, you just didn't *want* to see it. But even though these negative emotions can blind us in certain areas of our lives, if we turn the tables and seek out these emotions, they can often be wonderful clues to us. In other words, if there's something you're afraid of doing that's related to your dream somehow, you should probably do that thing.

Yeah, *that* thing. Mmmhm! You know the one. It's okay, you won't die. Probably.

Another way that you might identify your leap of faith, is to think about your big dream from a completely logical, strategic planning perspective, and then ask yourself what the fastest way to achieve your Big Dream is. Build an ambitious plan for yourself. Then deduce the activities or actions that will get the next needed result as fast as possible. Select the task at the top of your priority list (not the thing that is most comfortable), and move towards that. This will inevitably lead you to a point where you realize that the top of your list requires making some very big sacrifices and committing in a very big way.

When searching for your next leap of faith, you can not rely on other people to tell you exactly what your leap of faith is. Mentors can help you identify it by asking questions and making suggestions, but you're the only one who truly knows what your leap of faith needs to be. You're the one who is responsible for your dream, after all.

Whatever the details of your next leap of faith, you will know when you find it because it will resonate deeply with you. If you face your dream with resolution to take your leap, then you will find it with a mix of feeling overwhelmed and peacefully knowing that it is the best and only way forward for you. As cliche as it sounds, *you'll know when you find it.*

Your leaps of faith will come in all shapes and sizes. Some will help you to spend time outside of your comfort zone, and others will launch your Big Dream past the point of no return. Whether the next leap that you need to take is moving across the country to join forces with an organization, auditioning for your dream musical, or picking up the phone and calling someone, what really matters is that you do it.

The most important part of all this is that you jump into the lake when you find yourself standing on the edge of a cliff; when your leap shows up, you've gotta take it! As a matter of fact, that's exactly the next step to unveiling the rest of your next mission. The sixth step to discovering your dream, is **Take Your Leap.**

It's only a matter of time until you run into your leap of all leaps. In this critical moment of your journey, you will not be able to progress towards your dream until you face your fears and doubts, and jump with everything you have. If you do jump, you will hurtle towards the success and completion of your dream with breathtaking speed.

A leap of faith actually has an enormous amount of power to enable you to live your dream. It sets you and your dream on a path for success in two main ways: (1) it gives you momentum and propels you forward with massive action, and (2) it proves to yourself and everyone in the world that you're serious about your dream – that there's no turning back.

A leap of faith, done right, automatically benefits you in these two ways because it requires serious commitment and sacrifice from you. The presence of serious commitment and sacrifice is enough to weed out the people who are truly prepared for their dream, and those who are not yet willing to give what it takes. Once you take that big risk, you'll be moving forward fast, with no easy way to backtrack. Anyone who has compared falling off a cliff to climbing up it can attest that the analogy holds strong.

Some of you may, at this point, be wondering how taking a leap of faith to live your dream is going to help you find it. Since this does look primarily like a step towards achievement, not discovery, that's a fair question. The honest truth is, taking your leap is an absolutely critical step towards finding your dream and figuring out what the heck you want to do with your life.

Not only is your dream found in the living of it, but like we discussed in chapter five, your dream does not become a Complete Dream until after you've seen a Big Dream through to the end. Through the required commitment and sacrifice, your big leap of faith will ensure that your dream survives long enough to keep growing. If you don't take your leap when the time is ripe, the Big Dream that you once had will begin to fade away until the timeframe you have been given to achieve that specific mission has expired. At that point, you'll only be left with fragments of the Big Dream that once burned brightly within you. You'll then have to start the process over with an Awakening Dream.

A leap of faith is also a necessary step in your dream growth because it makes the intangible idea of your Big Dream real. You can't fully understand a truth until you live it. A dream that has not been seriously committed to and sacrificed for remains as only a vision of possibility. You didn't pick up this book to find hope. You came to find a mission.

I don't mean to say that all is lost if you feel captive by fear and doubt, and that if you've stepped away from a leap of faith once, your dream is done for. What I intend to get across is that your leap is a critical opportunity for you to take advantage of. It's an opportunity for you to massively explode the caliber of your Big Dream, grow into a new and more powerful dreamer, and start helping people in bigger ways than ever before. And if you've found a Big Dream, your leap is also the next mile marker along the road of your dream.

If you're not sure if now is the time for you to take a leap of faith, that's okay! Keep moving towards your dream, and the appropriate cliff will find you in no time. For now, start practicing your jump; live by faith, and live big. The right opportunity for your radical commitment and sacrifice will come soon enough.

LIONHEART GETS SERIOUS

Along the path to my dream, I have become well acquainted with leaps of faith. It has been my privilege and responsibility to have taken many such leaps, and I know that I will face many more as I continue to grow and dream. There is one leap of particular note, however, that I want to share with you. I took this leap beside two of my best friends, one month after a lighthouse moment graduated my life plan to the Big Dream level. It stands as the single greatest leap of faith I have encountered within the scope of my dream to lead the world of youth towards an embodiment of their true potential.

After my transformational moment of talking with God at that three day seminar, I continued taking whatever action I could to make that dream come into existence – only this time with even more resolve, and some fine-tuned clarity on where to focus my energy. The fire that drove me towards my mission had been stoked anew, and I was bound and determined to make this dream a reality.

I wasn't alone in this quest, either. My friends and partners Dallin and Quiana not only shared the Lionheart dream, but they were equally on fire about doing whatever it took to achieve it. We knew that this Big Dream was – is – desperately needed in the world, and that if we didn't get the ball rolling, no one would. The going was slow at first, but as we plowed forward by contacting schools, building mentoring curriculum, and establishing a primitive online presence, we began to attract a few fans who wanted to help us.

(One of the most useful attributes of a Big Dream is that because a Big Dream is larger than you are, there is room for other dreamers. Once a dream graduates to that level, that's when you really start putting together a dream team, and when you stop fighting for it all alone. But I digress.)

Now, on a cloudy February morning, we sat down at for a very important meeting in the lobby of a fast food restaurant. It wasn't the prime business meeting location for sure, but for a handful of teenagers, it would do just fine.

First we reviewed what we had done since the birth of our organization. We talked about our website and marketing attempts, we talked about the advice mentors had given us, we talked about the content we had created and we talked about the hundreds of people we had contacted. We had never done this before, but we assumed that since things were theoretically going somewhere, these were a good signs.

High fives.

Next we looked at our dream. Then back at our progress. Then back at our dream. We realized that although we had been doing a lot of things right, we needed to do something different if we were going to achieve the real purpose of our dream. We needed to do something BIGGER. More outside of the box and totally new. Something that we and only we could do to rock the youth of our world.

What makes us at Lionheart specially and uniquely equipped to achieve our Big Dream, is the fact that we teach and lead youth *while we are still youth*. We don't tell teenagers that they have potential from the perspective of an older adult; we are living embodiments of the principles we teach. When we got talking, it became obvious to us that our next step would be to start holding our own seminars, much like the ones that had been so impactful over the years for us. Youth leading seminars for youth wasn't something we had seen anywhere else, but it was a perfect fit for us!

We pulled up a calendar and scouted out dates. We didn't feel like the time was ripe to do a three day seminar just yet; it would be best if we started out with a short, highly inspiring evening event. We settled on the February 26, 2016, a little over three weeks away.

"This is going to be great!" we thought. Besides, it was the most logical course of action, so what was there to worry about? It just made sense.

A few days went by, and we were busily drawn in many directions and consequently did basically nothing to make our event happen. A week passed. Then two weeks. A fateful moment came when we suddenly woke up the fact that our first big seminar was only a handful of days away, and we had done nothing to launch it! We frantically started searching all over for venues to hold the event at, but couldn't find one to fit our needs. Our event was in trouble.

How can we change the world, I worried, *if we can't even motivate ourselves to create a single event?*

I know now that there was a simple reason for our lack of "motivation," and it's not really motivation at all that was the issue. We were in unfamiliar territory, trying to do something we knew almost nothing about, and sensing that our task carried great social risk. Although we had "decided" to do the event, we hadn't burned our boats yet.

None of us would have admitted it at the time, but we were afraid and at a loss for how to move forward. It was much easier to let other things consume our time and focus. As we stood near the edge of our cliff, we suddenly found the geological formations very fascinating. We found distraction in examining those rocks as long as we could, but there came a point where we could run no longer. We had to make a choice – a serious one now.

When the 8th day before the event rolled around, I was ready to say that we should give up on the project altogether. I distinctly remember talking on the phone with Dallin that day while crashed on my bed.

"Should we even do it?" I asked. We hadn't announced the event or paid for a venue, so we could reschedule without anyone noticing or losing any money. I had spoken to Quiana a few minutes earlier, and she was on the fence like I was.

Dallin and I were verbally weighing the pros and cons of doing the event on that day, given our situation. As we spoke, doubt weighed me down, and although I attempted to speak and contribute to our debate logically, a part of me really, really hoped we could just postpone the event and walk away from this obstacle.

It was a pivotal moment for us, our movement, the lives of thousands of youth, and for me. More than I ever could have guessed was riding on our decision. But without a place to hold the event, that decision seemed already made for us.

Almost, that is.

We did see one small shot at success. We found a single high school auditorium that would be sufficient for our needs, and was open for us to use. It seated eight hundred people and would cost us a total of over $1,000 for the evening in question. It was a shot, but taking that shot would require a serious sacrifice.

At the time, I was the only one with the cash on hand to sponsor the event. I don't know about you, but as a seventeen year old, I thought a thousand dollars was a big sum to spend on an event, especially with the possibility of it being sub-par due to the lack of time for marketing, logistics, and content production. Just think of how many hours I had to work at my minimum wage job to earn that amount! Not only that, but in an auditorium that seated eight hundred people, we would have to literally get hundreds of people to show up simply to prevent the audience feeling dwarfed by the size of it all.

Typically when you hold an event, the rule of thumb is that people need to have time to plan for the event and work it into their schedules in order for them to come. And here we were demanding of ourselves an audience of eight hundred people on a few days notice, never having hosted a large scale event before! In one word, we were *CRAZY*, and although we didn't have a good understanding of the actual difficulty of what we were trying to do, we could feel the recklessness of it weighing us down. This was an event planner's nightmare, and we were within seconds of walking away from such an irresponsible attempt.

"...but if we're actually going to do this, we've got to do it now." My voice was laced with doubt and worry. Although the phone connection surely masked some of that, I hoped Dallin would make a compelling case for why it would be wise to take another course of action. To regroup and plan ahead better. To face this obstacle some other day. His voice too was stressed and worried, but he did not grant my inward request.

"Yeah, you're right," he said. "I think we've just got to stick it out and make it happen."

My heart dropped, but I knew he was right. We could not afford a forever of "later"'s.

We hung up having made a decision to stick with the plan. We were going for it. This decision was a turning point for all three of us, but I'll let Dallin and Quiana speak for themselves. I made a choice that day to stare down the edge, and charge towards it. I chose to take my leap.

It might just be the single best decision I have ever made in my life.

I called Quiana back and explained the situation to her.

"I remember that when you first called me," she recalls, "I thought you were crazy. One of the things about events that had been emblazoned into my brain is that you needed to give people time to plan in advance. We were arguing, kind of going back and forth, and then I realized:

"Yeah, this is crazy. But isn't that what we're all about? Isn't the impossible something we just...Do?

"So I finally agreed."

After my conversation with Quiana, I called the venue and confirmed that we wanted to use it. The next seven days were lost to us in a sea of *pushing* the event forward. It was encompassed by a mad rush to use social media, email, calling and texting to tell everyone we possibly could about the event.

As Quiana would later recall regarding those days, "I had no idea what I was going to say. But I do remember getting on Facebook and watching the number of people interested in the event climb, and see the views of our video reach into the thousands. It was insane."

For me, it was one of the most simultaneously faithful and anxiety filled weeks I have ever had! The financial sacrifice I was making, along with the fact that we were putting ourselves and our new organization's reputation on the line, was stressing me out like nobody's business!

The day after we decided to go all out, I pulled together a friend's quiet living room and a camera. Quiana and I then recorded a video announcing the event, and everything it stood for. It would stand as a testament that teenagers could do incredible things, and that they didn't have to live lives of apathy, we said. It would help the attendees double their personal power so they could live more productive and exciting lives, we declared. What's more, we needed their help, because we were going to do something "impossible." We were going to fill every single one of those eight hundred seats!

I hurriedly edited the footage, and published it on social media for all the world to see. We were public. There was no easy turning back now.

We were running to the edge.

Three days later I paid the $1,000 fee for the venue. We were fully committed now. I knew it was the right course of action, but *man*, I sure found myself praying that it would work out. The venue paperwork turned out to be a mess, and with the time it would take for administration to process it, there was a possibility that it wouldn't go through in time. That was not good for our cause! Our situation was chaos, but we had chosen to make it work, and despite all the terror, we could feel a deep reassurance that everything would work out in the end.

The last days before the event were spent madly advertising the event everywhere that we could possibly think of, pulling together logistics, filling out more paperwork, finding a couple of volunteers to help us out the day-of, and a *lot* of pep-talking each other. We knew that Big Dreams were a lot to take in, but this was far from what we had anticipated. Before we knew it, the event was upon us.

When the day of February 26th arrived, we couldn't help but think to ourselves, "This is it!" Dallin and I drove to Quiana's house a few hours before we needed to set up for the event, and we sat down to review who was speaking at what times and whether or not our content would fit together appropriately. (Side note to all aspiring speakers out there: *don't wait until the day of your event to decide what's going to happen at it.* Unless of course you're in the middle of a leap of faith and have no idea what you're doing…in that case, carry on. You'll figure it out.)

We rehearsed for about two hours, then packed our cars with the stuff that we needed and drove to Lone Peak High School, a few minutes north of Provo, UT. Once we arrived, it was a mad rush to set up tables for check-in, projectors, decorations, and to work with the auditorium tech manager to get our sound system set up.

By 6:40p people started trickling into the event. Slowly at first, and then in a crowd. Thankfully, we had the insight to ask three of our friends to help us staff the check-in tables, because we were still running around trying to get little details figured out. It felt like things were barely being held together by our force of will.

Finally, we had everything in place.

The time was 7:04, and we needed to start the event. Technically we were already a few minutes late, but we figured that people would forgive us for being a few minutes off schedule, especially since they were continuing to arrive. Dallin, Quiana and I, with mics taped to our resolute faces, grabbed each other and moved outside the auditorium for a quick pow-wow. We stepped into an adjourning hall and huddled in a circle, arms around each other.

We looked at each other for a moment with expressions that seemed to say, "Well, I guess we're actually *doing this*."

It felt like we were being swept by a wave of our own creation towards something big, and although we could hardly believe it, we knew without a doubt that this was our time to shine. We were far from perfectly prepared, but we trusted in each other, and in our joint ability to overcome any obstacle. The time for performance had come, and we could not back down.

We said a brief prayer of gratitude, then put our hands together and at the count of three bellowed our warcry. The sound of "LIONHEART!" echoed through the high school hallways with a volume that surprised me. With that, we headed for the stage. We threw open the auditorium doors to reveal the waiting crowd, and began our first miraculous event.

We we had lept, and were now hurtling off the edge.

When was the last time you felt truly alive? As we live our lives, it's more than easy to slip into tracks of unconscious habit where we feel content, but slightly "bleh". Times when life is good, but it's nothing mindblowing.

Then there are other moments in life, ones that shake our world, and change us – sometimes for good, sometimes for bad. Regardless of how they affect us, we remember these moments as major milestones in our story. A leap of faith is one of the best of those moments that you can ever have. It's not something traumatic or thrilling that happens *to you*, but something triumphant that *you choose to create*.

Your leap of faith can be one of the greatest moments of your life (right alongside all the other milestones of your big dream). You will count it as one of the greatest moments of your life, because in that moment you will be living greatly! You may be encompassed about with a storm of concerns, but with those concerns comes a wave of possibility and the thrill of choosing to do something that has never been done before by you, or perhaps by anyone!

You are taking a big risk to move towards your dream. The outcome will be written in the history of your life as a glorious moment of success, learning, or both! And the very experience itself we be remembered as a grand adventure, just like the ones you've always dreamed of. You will be choosing to live freely, unconditionally, and with nothing held back!

In those moments, you can't help but be *alive*.

If there's one thing that Dallin, Quiana and I felt the second we stepped onto our stage, it was a feeling of being totally alive. From there the event was a blur. Our crowd was one hundred and seventy-five people strong – far from our goal of eight hundred, but we scarcely took time to consider that fact. They looked happy to be there, and we felt like they were the best audience in the world.

"The entire time, I had a feeling similar to panic," Quiana told me, "and a voice that ran through my head screaming, 'We're doing this. We're really doing this. This is real.' I remember that I was very unsure of myself....I didn't feel ready. I didn't feel competent. But I was on the stage and I *loved* it.

"I can't really remember what I said that night," she continued, "but I can remember the energy that filled the room once we all stepped off it. I knew that it had all been worth it. And I knew this was something I wanted to do for forever."

Quiana, Dallin, and I were on top of the world as the event progressed. At the end of our ninety minute seminar, we were enveloped by feelings of relief, gratitude, and pure triumph! Not everything was perfect that night, and we sure didn't have eight hundred people there, but our event was everything we could have hoped for and more. Our leap of faith had been a resounding success!

Not only did our event help us spread the word about our movement, and not only did it make a difference in the lives of some of the people who attended, but Dallin, Quiana and I walked away from it fundamentally and permanently changed for the better. The dedication and audacity we displayed at that event pulled people to us, fans and supporters alike. What's more, the pattern of commitment and sacrifice we established through that event was absolutely critical for the survival and ultimate victory of our Big Dream: it enabled us to slave away full time in my basement for months as we experimented with programs and events, with failure after failure, lesson after lesson, small success after small success, before we finally created a steady movement.

We probably could have started things small and grown systematically with the right strategy in place to get the results we needed – assuming we could have found that strategy. But a leap of faith isn't just about getting results. It's about committing and sacrificing. We stepped up to the level of our Big Dream. Without having done that, we *never* would have left the ground.

As for me personally, choosing to take my big leap of faith changed my heart. I walked away knowing that I, a frequently-arrogant and insensitive young man, could touch the lives of other people. I knew this dream really, truly mattered. I thought I understood that before, but now I truly *knew*. It was real for me, and the thought of giving anything less than my best for this dream was incomprehensible.

In that moment I wasn't too worried if I could be good enough for my dream and to bring light and love to people. I still had much to learn (and still do), but I had passed the test. The evidence I assumed through faith was now manifesting before me.

I had a dream. *We* had a dream. And nothing would stop us from honoring it.

HOW TO JUMP

Facing the need to take a leap of faith can feel like an impossible task, especially when you don't have as clear a picture of what leaping looks like as you would if you were jumping off a literal cliff into a lake. As a dreamer who is closely acquainted with leaps of faith, let me teach you how to jump so that your leap is as powerful as it needs to be:

1. Jump with extreme clarity. Leaps of faith are only leaps of faith if you take a big risk that is a necessary next step to accomplishing your dream. We sincere dreamers aren't in the business of taking risks all over the place simply for the adrenaline rush alone (although I will admit that the thrill part of hurtling off the edge while taking a leap of faith does feel freakin' *awesome!*) What we do is more meaningful and important than that. You've got to have a clear understanding of why you're jumping and where you want to be.

So don't just rush up to the first scary cliff you can think of, just because I say you need to do something that involves pushing past doubt and fear; make sure it's the right cliff for you to be jumping off. If you can't see a leap that you need to take right now, don't worry about it. Keep moving towards your dream as fast as you can, and soon enough, you'll find the right one.

If you do know, deep within you, what leap you need to take, then "finding extreme clarity" doesn't mean procrastinating by taking a long time to figure out every last detail. It means that you face your options with the best knowledge you know how, listen carefully, and seek out your fears.

When your journey does lead you to a cliff's edge, it is imperative that you find extreme clarity on why you are standing up there. If you have certainty that your dream and a better you lie beyond the chasm of uncertainty, you will soon summon the courage to jump, no matter the odds. If you are unsure of what what you are seeking or who you are, you never will.

To figure out whether or not a leap is right for you, ask yourself these two questions:

Will I be limited in my ability to serve others through my dream if I walk away from this challenge?

Is this the most direct way for me to start achieving the results that my dream requires?

2. Jump with a champion team supporting you. Your leap of faith will put you under deep stress, and in most cases, you don't have to fight that battle on your own. It is your leap of faith, but there are many people who will support you and believe in you along the way, and celebrate with you after you have jumped. The success of your leap of faith could very well depend on your reaching out to these people – mine certainly did. Your champion team could look like your teachers and coaches, your close family members, your teammates or partners, or just a best friend who will get up at 6:00am and climb a sketchy outcropping of rock to set up a camera.

Whatever you do, make sure that you have at least two specific people on your champion team when you set out to conquer your leap of faith: the first person should be a mentor who has been down a similar path to that of your dream. This person will guide you through some specific steps you need to take and give you invaluable advice. The second person, should be a buddy. This is the person who will walk every step with you, right up to the edge (and give you a loving push if needed).

In your Dream Journal, jot down two names: *Who do I know of who would be the perfect mentor for me through this leap of faith, and who would make a great wingman?*

3. Move TODAY. One of the saddest feelings in the world is waking up one day to realize that your golden opportunity – perhaps the fire of your dream itself – has burned out. That sad story is the danger of what happens when dreamers procrastinate their big leap. Don't let that happen to you! Once you see your leap, charge towards it and do not wait! Opportunity waits for no one, not even your well-dressed, fast-talking excuses. Do not take the greatest risk of all by delaying your dream for lesser things.

Make the choice to never back down from a leap of faith that you know you need to take. If there's a leap of faith looming in your future, then take actions now to prepare for it, and move towards it with faith. If you're standing on the edge of the cliff with sufficient clarity, jump!

Some people run away from this moment. They're terrified that things will fail, and that they will look bad, that their dream is just too far out of their league, and therefore that they aren't cut out for the life of a dreamer. That is not you!

The honest truth is, things will never be as bad as you fear them to be. *Even if they are,* the alternative to jumping is to hide from your dream. To shrink from your mission. To lock your quest away somewhere where it will slowly dwindle until it ceases to exist. That is to choose the greatest and most deadly risk I can think of. That, my friend, is *not living at all*.

4. Hold nothing back. If you've ever jumped off a cliff, you know that it's an all or nothing game. If you reject Yoda's sage advice to "Do or do not," and half heartedly take your leap of faith, your worst fears of embarrassment, failure, and skidding down a massive rock have their highest likelihood of coming true. But even if you crash and burn, that pain will pale in comparison to the pain of knowing that in the face of a great opportunity, you held yourself back and didn't give it your all.

When faced with your leap of faith, you will be tempted to take an easier road. For what you're looking for, an easier way simply is not sufficient. One will definitely exist in some form or another, but you will know in your heart that it is a comfortable, but cheap counterfeit. After you take your leap, you will agree that an easier way would have been nowhere near as fun, either!

Commit to your leap fully and ambitiously, with nothing held back. "All in" is the name of your game. The bigger the leap you take, the further you'll progress on your dream, and the more committed you'll prove yourself to be.

For example, let's say that you're terrified of large audiences, but you want to be a singer and share your vocal gifts with the world. You know that your leap of faith will involve organizing a recital showcasing you as a singer. You might be tempted to invite a few close family members and friends over to your house and sing a song or two. Crush that temptation. Instead, rent out an auditorium; advertise all over your city; prepare a full show; get a team to help you.

Do not concern yourself with plan B's and C's – things will work out for you even if your worst fears come true. You have the strength and brilliance to figure things out on the other side of the cliff. It doesn't take a hero to do something "realistic" or "safe," so go all out.

For some things in life, it works okay to ease yourself slowly into progress. Not for leaps of faith! This is your Big Dream we're talking about, and it deserves more than that! By playing it safe, you will set a precedent of mediocrity that can cripple your personal power. You need to train yourself such that when you play, you play BIG! Anything less will not enable you to live your dream to it's fullest potential.

DO I HAVE THE STRENGTH TO JUMP?

When you stand on the edge of the cliff and stare down at the leap ahead, you brain will probably tell you that you'll be fine. Your emotions will be asking an entirely different question:

"Am I strong enough for this?"

It's a fair question, one that only you can, and must answer. Anyone who has faced a leap of faith on the path to their Big Dream knows exactly how you feel, because we've had to ask ourselves a variation of that same question many, many times.

If you're currently standing on the edge of a cliff, too terrified to jump or too worried about what *could* happen if things go amiss, then I invite you to pay close attention to the story I'm about to share with you. I believe it will help you find the strength you're looking for.

Remember how your dream is built to serve and bless the lives of others? I have a friend who understood that principle by heart. His name is David.

David and I worked together for three seasons of competitive mock trial at the High School level. If you've never heard of mock trial, it's a lot like speech and debate, except that your team is issued a full blown fictional court case, and you study the witness statements and courtroom procedures before arguing your side of the case against opposing teams in the courtroom. In those three seasons we won our way to the state championship twice, becoming a tight knit team in the process.

At five foot eight, about one hundred and twenty pounds, and with a young face, David didn't look very big or intimidating, but he was passionate, caring, and sincere. He looked out for others, and we shared a love for mock trial. He had found his purpose in teaching others and spreading messages of light and freedom to them, and so, after our last season of mock trial together and the end of high school, he set out to live that purpose in a big way. The last time I saw David was the day we fought for the state championship the second time.

In the summer of 2015, David packed his things and set off on a teaching mission for the LDS Church with a duration of two years. After weeks of bootcamp-level preparation and study, he was sent to Taiwan and began the intense work of finding and sharing with others about Jesus Christ and his teachings. Every day he got up at 6:30am, studied intensely, did a short workout, got his stuff together, and walked out the door with another young man living in Taiwan for the same purpose. They walked the streets, knocked doors, and spoke to everyone who would listen before crashing into bed at 10:30 at night.

Neither David nor his companion were native speakers of Mandarin, and that fact coupled with the relentless nature of their work made his situation far from easy! But did that matter? No! He was changing lives, and bringing joy and freedom to people!

Back at home, I was proud of David, and was happily receiving the news he sent home to friends and family. We were all happy for David! He was living a very important Big Dream, and was exactly where he needed to be.

Then one day, the unthinkable happened.

I was sitting at my desktop computer, working on a school assignment. My phone buzzed and I picked it up, casually swiping to read the new text. In shock and disbelief I reread the message many times before slumping in my chair and staring blankly at the wall. David had only been away from home for a grand total of four months. I had just learned that he, while traveling via his bike through a busy and crowded street on the other side of the planet, had fallen from his bike into traffic, hit by a car, and killed.

He was only 18 years old.

I hope you will take two lessons from David's story. The first, is that life is too short to live in fear. Every moment you let fear dictate your actions is a moment of lost potential. Instead, dedicate your life to living by faith. Faith doesn't require you to impulsively jump at every reckless opportunity, it simply says that if there's something you know you should do, you're committed to trusting yourself and to trusting the greater source of light from which your Big Dream has come.

Fear and doubt make lists of everything that could go wrong, immobilizing your ability to act. Faith doesn't need a list, because it trusts that everything will turn out alright in the end; such faith is the foundation for all action, and it is yours to choose. My close friend and fellow mentor at Lionheart, Ethan Fausett, put it this way: "Faith and fear are both equally rational. One of them is just a lot more useful."

So if you only have one life to live, and that life could end when you least expect it, why waste time giving power to your fear?

I don't mean to worry you with the thought that you'll die at any moment, not at all. The point is not to worry about all the moments we do not have, but to take responsibility for the moments that we *do* have; to be a wise steward of those moments by using them to honor our true selves and our Big Dreams. Fear and doubt – the bullies on the edge of your cliff – would have you trade the most important adventures of your life for moments of temporary comfort. You have been given the precious gift of life. Choose to live by faith!

The second lesson of this story comes from the mouth of David himself. While he was away, David would write weekly letters back to friends and family at home. At the end of every letter, his signature was accompanied by a saying that would be memorialized after his death:

"It's not about you."

At the end of your life, when your time for living Big Dreams here on this planet is over, you're going to look back and realize that the greatest question you will have for your yourself is whether you loved the people who surrounded you. We are here on this earth to give, serve and love. If you miss the mark on that, I believe you'll find few other things can bring you to say that you lived a life to be proud of.

When Dallin stood on the edge of the forty foot cliff that August morning, he wasn't about to dive in for fun. He was there because he knew that he had fears and doubts that were holding him back, and that if he didn't break through those fears and doubts, *he would severely limit his ability to help others.* It was his failure to assist his friend's Operation Underground Railroad campaign that led him there in the first place. He was jumping for his own growth, but at the same time, it wasn't about him. If it was about him, he would have taken an easier path – the terror I saw on his face assures me of that.

At the peak of your doubts, insecurities, and fears, you must remember why you began this journey in the first place. You are a dreamer. You have been given a mission to live, one that only you are fully capable of achieving. Other people need you to lead! While your Big Dream is a gift to you, it is also a gift to others.

It's not about you. It never was. The moment your Big Dream becomes about you, is the moment that your purpose fades and you begin to lose heart and strength at the sight of your leap of faith. Yes, you must trust in yourself. Yes, you must have confidence. But those are only the beginning. If you want to have the strength to face anything, you must ultimately lose yourself in valiant service to others.

If you are being called to do a work that will uplift, liberate, or bless others – even if that only looks like taking major steps to learn and grow yourself right now – then DON'T YOU DARE BACK DOWN!

Don't you *dare* walk away from your cliff and live as a slave to fear and doubt!

It's time for you to take the leap; to live like never before.

In your Dream Journal, write down your next leap of faith, and a date that you commit to taking it by. Call up your mentor and buddy figures, and tell them about it. Ask for their support, and tell them that you're not backing away from your next leap, no matter what.

Once you're in and committed, you start truly *living.*

What are you waiting for?

The 7 Steps to Discovering Your Dream:

1. CHOOSE TO SEEK YOUR DREAM

If you want to find your dream, you need to deliberately search for it. Make the intentional choice to become a dreamer. Naysayers will call this process risky, but the greatest risk is never living at your highest potential. Decide that the answer to what YOU want to do with your life will be found by discovering your dream.

2. KNOW WHAT YOU'RE LOOKING FOR

The more clearly you can define what you want, the more direct your path to obtaining it will be. Study the principles and formulas that characterize dreams. Write out your life purpose. Reflect on your passions, aptitudes, and the needs of the world. Take the time to decide how you'll know YOUR dream when you find it.

3. FREE THE HERO WITHIN

You can't find your dream until you have taken responsibility for your life. It takes a hero to live a dream. Choose to learn of, and believe in, your divine worth and potential. Stop holding yourself back. Instead, give yourself permission to be great.

4. PAY THE PRICE FOR YOUR DREAM

Discovering your dream is as much a journey as achieving it. Sometimes, all you can see is one small step ahead. Get clear about what that next step is, and take it. It will move you in the direction of further clarity. The best way to ensure that you don't figure out what your dream is, is to sit around and wait for it to show up.

5. SUBMIT YOUR DREAM TO SOMETHING GREATER

Because a Big Dream is greater than you, it must ultimately come from a greater source. After you have paid the price for your dream, you must be willing to give it all up in exchange for something better. Trust the greatest source of light and wisdom you can find. When the time is right, your trust will be answered with a glorious mission for you to fulfil.

6. TAKE YOUR LEAP

Your dream will become real the moment you take an audacious leap of faith. Your leap of faith will ensure the survival of your dream and propel you forward with the momentum of results. Commit to your dream. Sacrifice for your dream. Take the big risk. Doing so will enable you to serve others in a greater way than ever before.

Seven

LIVING A MIRACLE

Often miracles are happening right in front of our eyes...but we think they should look different, so we miss them even though they're right there.
~ Marianne Williamson.

The night of our first big Lionheart event, we weren't the only ones at the edge of a metaphorical cliff. Unbeknownst to us, as we ran towards our "impossible" seminar, a girl by the name of Grace was taking a leap of faith of her own. It wasn't the leap of faith one takes to cement a Big Dream, but rather, one that would determine something even more fundamental in her journey.

Now eighteen years old, Grace is a Lionheart mentor, and has led the movement in important ways over the last year and a half. I'm not only proud to know her, but I'm also excited to see her dream fully become a reality:

"My dream is to start a rehab ranch (called Healers Cove) for people who struggle with suicide, eating disorders, and sexual abuse," she wrote to me. "But right now, my dream is to show up for the broken ones (whom I love) so that they can exceed all expectations that they have of themselves, by discovering that they are unconquerable and have unconquerable souls." She speaks excitedly and often of her vision for this ranch, and when the time is right, I know she's going to build something phenomenal.

Grace has had this dream for years. Since the age of 13, actually. It was a need that she saw in the world, something she knew she could help with. But there came a day when it didn't matter at all.

Like far too many teenagers, Grace was bullied. It started small, by some of her close classmates at school who banished her from certain social groups. To those who know her well, Grace is a fiercely caring, positive person with tons of energy by nature, and this deliberate rejection got her down. Like, way down. She had unconsciously given her personal worth away to these friends, and when they turned traitorous, it took a nasty blow.

If the actions of her classmates weren't bad enough, Grace was kicked out of her small private school because one of the teachers didn't feel like it was the best place for Grace to learn. The rumors increased, and the bullying got worse. Grace began experiencing severe challenges with anxiety and depression. Each of her closest friends left her, and some took part in the bullying. In her words, "The real me was being brutally hit and beaten, and I let her die."

Grace continued living in this dark pit for over a year, until she decided that she couldn't stand it any longer. No, her dream didn't matter to her any more. How could it, when all she saw was that her gifts, her efforts, and who she was as a person didn't matter to other people? With the negativity and pain becoming more and more prominent in her life, she couldn't even find a compelling reason to keep on living.

In her lowest point, a random friend whom she hadn't talked to in weeks sent her a text: "Hey, I'm actually going to that Lionheart event tonight. Do you want to sit by me?"

Grace had heard about our event, but decided that she wasn't going to attend. It was 6:00pm when her friend texted her, and with an hour drive, it looked like they would be a few minutes late to the event. That was one reason not to go. Besides, it was put on by a bunch of teenagers – which was cool, she had to admit, but what did they have to say that could change her miserable life?

It was then that Grace realized that she didn't have anything to lose. Her life already wasn't worth living, so it couldn't get any worse. *It won't make a difference anyways, but what the heck,* she thought. *Why not. I'll go.*

At the seminar, Dallin, Quiana, and I had no way of knowing what Grace was going through. We had no idea what anyone in the audience was going through, honestly; we rarely ever do. Part of the dream of helping people change their lives through these types of events is that some people come in critical moments of their life, and others come because they are bored. As a facilitator, you just do your thing and you don't always know who you're going to seriously influence.

As Grace sat in the audience, she noted that the teenage speakers before her actually seemed to have something going for them. I, for one, was having the time of my life! I loved being on stage, I was sharing principles and techniques that would really help people, and I was watching my friends and partners be brilliant and do the same. Over the course of our ninety minute seminar, Dallin or Quiana would pass me the stage, I welcomed the thunderous applause, enthusiastically sharing stories and teaching principles, I would then pass it right back to one of them, they would rock the stage, and we would repeat!

Right in the middle of the event, I decided to do something big for someone in the audience. I didn't know if it would quite work the way I wanted it to, but at this point in our leap of faith the word "risk" had basically lost all meaning to me. I was talking about limitations we live with as a result of false and damaging beliefs about ourselves that we adopt throughout our life (identity garbage), and I asked for everyone to reflect and identify a belief that was holding them back. Hands went up. I asked for a volunteer to join me on stage and break through that belief in front of everyone. Hands went down.

My eye fixed upon a girl with her hand still raised, sitting at the very back of the crowd. She was wearing a grey sweatshirt and a maroon beanie. I called on her and invited her up on stage, really hoping that I had picked the right person.

I asked her what her name was. It was Grace.

Standing there next to me, she was noticeably shaking all over. I gently put my arm around her. I asked her a few questions and invited her to share some things, carefully walking her through a powerful breakthrough process designed to free the hero within. There was scarcely a dry eye in the room as we witnessed her tell everyone about how she had given away her happiness and worth to other people. With Dallin and Quiana supportively flanking us on the stage, I told Grace that she didn't have to live like that, and I invited her to make a new choice regarding her happiness. Right then and there, she chose to reclaim it!

With some coaxing, Grace clutched the microphone tightly, and holding it to her lips, declared, "I AM ENOUGH. AND I CAN CHANGE THE WORLD!" The audience exploded. They were touched by the vulnerability, and enthusiastically affirmed her new choice.

I wasn't originally planning on including that breakthrough exercise in the middle of my presentation, but over the last twenty four hours I had felt a soft impression to do so. As I noted the impact it had on the audience and excused Grace from the stage with a hug, I thought to myself:

Sweet! That actually turned out really well. I'm glad it didn't flop!

If only I could have known just how much it hadn't "flopped"!

After the event we were approached by many people who wanted to congratulate and praise us. Many thanked us for the life-changing experience they had, and some said they wanted to get involved with what we were doing.

I was wrapping up a conversation with a handful of youth when one girl pushed through the rest of them. She was wearing a sweatshirt and a beanie.

"Hey, Grace!" I said. With a look of gravity and importance, she pulled me aside and looked up at me.

"I want you to know… that you saved my life." I blinked and my jaw dropped half an inch, not quite comprehending.

"My plan was to overdose tonight or tomorrow morning," she continued. "Now I'm not going to. I'm going to be happy and I choose to live." I gave her the biggest hug I could.

The full reality of what she had said didn't really hit me until after we had cleaned up the event, kicked everyone out, tipped the A/V guy who was managing the school auditorium, packed our cars and locked the doors. Dallin, Quiana and I were the last ones to leave, and we circled up once more in the empty parking lot. The stars were beautiful and the night quiet.

We had taken our leap, swam to shore, and could now take a long and relieved breath. It was hard to believe what we had just accomplished. In the course of seven days we – two eighteen-year-olds and a seventeen-year-old – had drawn together almost two hundred paying audience members to a self-improvement event to hear speakers (us) who had absolutely no name for themselves in the speaking/coaching world. We had done this with no official team, no marketing budget, and no experience. We then impressed our sceptics, changed lives, and created a name for ourselves.

To be fair, we and Lionheart Mentoring were *far* from the place we were destined to be, and the next year would be an intense battle to discover our place of maximum impact and hone our abilities. We weren't perfect on stage, we didn't know who our target audience was, we didn't know what our core messages should be, we didn't know how to be financially sustainable, and we didn't know where to focus our energy and time.

But through a leap of faith, we had started! Almost everyone in our social circles was now aware that we considered ourselves speakers and mentors. We had now built a following, we were beyond committed, and we knew that we could accomplish what others considered impossible!

The three of us stood outside on the sidewalk and took it all in. I was the only one who knew anything about Grace's leap of faith and the dire stakes we had helped her navigate. Dallin looked at Quiana and I.

"Well guys," he said matter of factly, "I think we definitely changed some lives tonight. Especially for Grace."

"According to her," I replied, "we also saved one."

Quiana muttered a soft "Wow."

The three of us stood there in partial disbelief about what we had just experienced. Our leap of faith had directly impacted hundreds of people, strengthened and trouched dozens of youth, and saved one girl's life. As we walked to our cars, we realized that while we had certainly done a noble deed by committing to our dream and making big sacrifices for its survival, there was so much that we did not, *could not* have ever controlled about our success that night.

So much had gone right that could have easily gone wrong. From the perspective of a detailed investigator, our seminar that night *should not* have happened like it did – or even at all. As someone who is now well familiar with the speaking a mentoring industry, I can confidently say that our event was absolutely unparalleled.

I've met a lot of public speakers, mentors, and youth leaders, and not one of them has started out anywhere close to how we did. One simply does not pull almost two hundred people to your very first, I'll-tell-you-how-to-live-a-better-life event, having essentially no name for yourself and no organizational sponsor. And if history is to be believed, you sure as heck don't do that as a teenager!

Thankfully, no one had told us that. Or if they did, we didn't listen to them. We believed in our limitless potential, and we had a Big Dream that we knew, without a shadow of a doubt, needed to be created in our world. So we dreamed audaciously, acted with diligence, and lept with complete faith.

But despite this diligent action and the preparation achieved through paying the price for our dream, I am convinced that we did not win this glorious triumph on our own. Yes, we were phenominal. But not *that* phenomenal. There was simply too much outside of our control that worked out for our benefit and the benefit of the people like Grace who needed our event to happen.

For starters, the venue paperwork was technically due weeks before the event happened. It was only because a lady working there had been hired only a few days before, and either wasn't sure what she was doing or bent some normal policies, that we were able to use the space.

Another example is the blatant fact that we had no control over who actually showed up to the event. They all chose to come for their own reasons. We couldn't control the number of people who showed up, and we couldn't control whether the people who really needed the event, like Grace, would hear about it in the first place. We also had no control over the people who thought our event was great enough to spread the word about it in their own ways.

Additionally, there was our performance at the event. With such little preparation, we could have easily have failed to deliver such high energy, focus, and organization. We happened to be completely on our best game that day, and we were prepared because of content we had learned from mentors that had recently showed up in our lives.

And who can forget all of the things that could have gone wrong? What if one of our cars had broken down on the way there and we couldn't show up on time? What if our video hadn't clicked with the right people? What if I hadn't had enough money in my bank account to pay for the venue? What if Grace's friend had gotten distracted by a new season on Netflix and never texted her? What Dallin had fallen sick with horrible food poisoning because he ate a suspicious looking burrito for lunch?

You smile, but these are all real possibilities. At least as real as the possibilities that actually happened. Had any of the contributing factors beyond our control gone differently, our event would not have been the same. In fact, it might not have happened at all! We influenced the outcome of our event, but the end results were far beyond our control. You can call us lucky, but we believe that a greater force was at work. As Dallin, Quiana, and I walked to our cars, we knew that we had intimately witnessed, and participated in, a miracle.

Yes, **a miracle**. The first of many miracles that we would behold, receive, or facilitate during our time living the Big Dream of

Lionheart.

I define a miracle as something that happens for the benefit of your purpose that you had no control over, nor expectation or knowledge of. A miracle is what happens when you do the right thing, not knowing how things will work out, and find that they do in the most perfect way possible. It's what happens when you take a leap of faith, and find your trust rewarded in a way that you didn't exactly plan for, yet at the same time, perfectly suits your needs and makes the next step of your mission possible.

> ## *Miracle*
>
> Something that happens for the benefit of your purpose that you had no control over, nor expectation or knowledge of.

For the last three years, I have been plagued with a question: how do you know, for sure, that you are living your dream?

The journey towards your dream prompts moments of failure, discouragement, and difficulty, just like it prompts moments of triumph, joy, and opportunity. As you strive to achieve a Big Dream, you may be tempted at times to question if you are truly living your dream, or if perhaps you're still missing something – if perhaps there is something bigger elsewhere that would feel even more like the mythical "live your dream" statements we so often hear about. How do you know what is an illusion of ease, and what is greater opportunity?

In short, how do I know if I'm living my dream?

After my time living my dream and teaching others how to do the same, I believe that I've finally found the answer: you look for the miracles.

Yes, when you're living your dream you'll often feel on fire about life. Yes, you'll face terrifying opportunities. Yes, you'll live the life of a hero. Yes, you'll get results and change lives. Those are all natural side effects of a dream. But the one consistent presence – through both thin and thin – that follows the journey of a hero fully committed to, and sacrificing for a Big Dream, is the presence of miracles.

Miracles pave the way for heroes like you and I to complete our dreams. If you are valiantly pursuing a Big Dream, you will also be living miracles. You won't always see them at first, and the going will frequently test your limits, but miracles will stand as mile markers along the path of your truest success.

The seventh and final step to discovering your dream, is **Look For The Miracles.** If miracles are happening, you're living your dream, and you're doing it right. If you go for too long without seeing miracles, then you need to change either the direction of your dream or your dedication to it.

This is the final step that you need to understand in order to fully uncover your Complete Dream, because it serves the purpose of guiding you from the acceptance of a Big Dream to its accomplishment. No one can pretend to map out everything you need to know to discover every detail of your dream, because the only person who will ever do that, is you. What this step can do, however, is help you know if you are where you are supposed to be. From there, you'll know exactly what to do next.

If you pay attention to the miracles, they will show you what is working and what is not. They will show you hidden opportunity. They will show you the work that you were born to do. Because who doesn't want to live a miraculous life?

COUNTING MIRACLES

The story of Lionheart is a story of miracles. The moment I truly understood this was about seven months following the event that served as our leap of faith. In that time, we had worked insanely hard, and struggled through the "grind" of polishing ourselves, our system, and our messages. Up until this moment, I hadn't been looking for the miracles.

One day, in preparation for an upcoming event, Dallin and I were rehearsing alone in the basement cave we called HQ. He was giving a kick-butt speech about how no matter the circumstances you face in your life, you always have a choice; with that choice, you can choose to be free. It was a staple speech of our events, and communicated a principle that we held dear to our hearts.

As his speech drew to a close, I sunk into my seat on the couch, overwhelmed with gratitude, as I considered the odds of what I was witnessing.

Of all the billions of people who have ever lived, how many of them understood the true power of personal agency to rise above all present circumstance? Millions, maybe.

Of all the people who understood that eternal truth, how many had the skills and opportunity to craft a beautiful, persuasive, transformational speech about it? Perhaps hundreds of thousands, if you're being generous.

Of all the people who have been prepared to do so, how many have set out on a personal mission to proclaim this truth and use it's power to lift others up? Thousands.

Of all the people living such a dream at such a young age, how many of them were (or are) teenagers? Not many. Possibly only a few hundred.

Now, my best friend and I had joined those ranks. Our movement brought internal freedom to others, but even if no one ever heard us speak, we were boldly standing for these truths. That moment of proclaiming the truths of personal freedom is the first and most important miracle of the Lionheart movement. If all our work was to enable one teenager – one person even – to stand alone in an empty auditorium and speak these truths of freedom, it would be worth it.

That moment was made possible because great men and women of the past had lived to discover the truths about freedom and because we had been born in the right time and place to learn from them, with the right teachers, the right natural aptitudes and interests, the right mentors and parents, the prosperity to hone our skills, the Big Dream to guide us, and the perfect companions to support us.

When any one of us chooses to stand for the principles of freedom, I count it as a miracle. It was after I realized this while rehearsing with Dallin that I began to look for the miracles of our dream. As I opened my eyes, they seemed to flood in. I now see miracles dancing with us throughout every moment that is core to our dream.

It is a miracle that Alex, a young man with a heart broken by shame, happened to show up to an event that we facilitators were worried was falling apart. We had hardly anyone in the audience, and miscommunication had created some minor chaos. When we moved into a symbolic board breaking activity, Alex chose to be vulnerable and opened up about his story. With tears running down his face, he perfectly united and transformed everyone in that intimate group. Far more importantly, he chose to forgive the young man who had become his own worst enemy.

It is a miracle that Daniel just so happened to be introduced to Quiana by a mutual teacher at a school social activity, and that when he heard about Lionheart, practically pried information about our next event from her. We had hit a low point where we were exhausted the audience of our close friends, and we didn't know what to do. Daniel started single handedly spiking our attendance rates by bringing new friends from school to a string of six consecutive events.

Not only did he champion those friends, but he also opened up a door of opportunity to us. His lead was followed by other youth who believed in our message, and wanted to see our movement grow. They would literally fill up their cars with their friends and drive them to our events. I cannot name them all, but they know who they are, and I consider them miracle workers.

It is a miracle that we always had enough money to keep going, even through our business was built and is completely run by teenagers with no business degrees and very little entrepreneurship experience. It was built on only $3,000 of personal savings in an industry where an inexpensive project will cost hundreds of dollars. Yet despite our inexperience, financial and legal requirements always managed to work out. They worked out even when we grew into 6 employees within the first two months of operation. They worked out even when we made a contractual mistake that nearly bankrupted us. They continue to work out even as responsibilities constantly shifts and we face new logistical challenges.

It is a miracle that the right youth have come to join our group of mentors. The Lionheart Mentors are the core leadership of our movement, and with the wrong leaders, our movement is toast. In our ambition to grow our dream as fast as possible, we sometimes felt discouraged when only a few youth decided to join our elite training program. But when I look at the group that currently exists,

I can't help but see that they are the perfect heroes for the task. The thousands of pivotal decisions that influenced each of them being here leaves me in awe.

It is a miracle that an unsolicited $2,000 scholarship showed up for one of our students and rising leaders. Grace was speaking at an entrepreneurship conference for women, when a lady raised her hand in the middle of Grace's presentation and announced that she was going to pay the way for a teenager in need to become one of our mentors. None of us were expecting anything like that to happen, and when it did, our jaws dropped – we had just such a student in mind, and we knew that the program would change his life. Grace hadn't even asked for a sponsor!

It is a miracle that Burke and Aaron, two of our loyal staff, have continued to serve at almost every single event we've had. They receive no pay for their efforts, but show up to lift heavy things, move chairs, take pictures, set up and take down our stuff, and pass out things throughout our seminars. They do this often at the expense of their Friday or Saturday evenings, I might add. Burke and Aaron, along with the other youth who have volunteered their time and energy for our movement, do so because they want to give and they know they can make a difference by pitching in.

It is a miracle that Ashlie's work shift was dropped just in time for her to show up to this strange thing called a "Lionheart event." She wasn't happy with her life or where it was headed, and being free to show up to the event triggered a course of events that, according to her, led her to change more as a person in the next four months than she had in the previous four years.

Ashlie is one of many youth who have felt a need to to attend one of our events, but previously couldn't because of other commitments. Opportunity always seems to align in just the perfect moment for them to change their lives in the way they have needed to, or for them to show up to make a difference in the life of someone else.

These are a few of the many miracles I have witnesses along the road to our Big Dream. Now, do all the people involved in these miracles consider them unexplainable, mind-bending, or extraordinary? Probably not. They would shrug and say that they just did what they could – which is true!

But from the perspective of the dreamer, they are still miracles. We have no control over their happening, and they benefit our purpose in huge ways. When God shrugs and says that He just did what He could, that doesn't make His work any less of a miracle.

The miracles of your dream might not seem mind-blowing at first glance, because unless you take the time to look for them, you might take them for granted or miss the incredible complexity and improbability of their existence. Regardless, they are there. If you look for them, you will see miracles, and they will teach you more and more about your dream.

My time on the road of dream discovery has led me to a blessedly empowering conclusion: *miracles do exist*. Whether you chalk them up to be the workings of the universe or the gift of Divine Providence, they are real.

WHERE ARE THE MIRACLES?

Are you ready to live miracles?

Your dream certainly qualifies you to do so. Dreams and miracles can be deeply intertwined if you're willing to position yourself properly to live them. Looking for the miracles will guide you the rest of the way down the path of discovering your dream because the miracles are indicators that you are living in alignment with your mission, and also that the *way* you are living your dream honors the priceless treasure you've discovered. Generally speaking, the more in alignment you are and the better you show up for your dream, the bigger your miracles will be.

Miracles are created when four things happen:

You are where you're supposed to be, doing what you're supposed to do.

You look at the future with complete, audacious faith

You work diligently, giving your best to the accomplishment of your mission

You accept the full measure of your truest and most glorious potential.

When you're living those four requirements, miracles will start showing up. And if miracles are showing up, you know you're living your dream. If miracles are consistently not showing up, you need to figure out why.

If you've accepted the call of a Big Dream, taken leaps of faith, and labored down the path of your dream, but you've stopped seeing miracles, then get out your Dream Journal. I have a very simple question for you to ask yourself:

"Who am I being to prevent miracles from happening?"

The absence of miracles has nothing to do with forces beyond your control or a problem with your dream. If miracles are absent, you need to take some solo reflection time to figure out what you need to change. You need to discover what you're doing, or not doing, that is preventing miracles from happening in the work of your dream or in the lives of those that are touched by it.

Is there something you need to change about what you're doing?

Are you exercising great faith?

Are you giving your best – your true best?

Have your forgotten who you are and what you're capable of?

If you're stuck without miracles, then there is simply something for you to change. Maybe you've lost sight of your Big Dream. Maybe you've unconsciously traded your dedication for comfort, money, disbelief, or any number of lesser things. Maybe you've become distant from the needs your dream is built to fill, and you've let it become about you.

In life, we fight a constant battle to remember who we are, what we stand for and what we really want from this world. The path of your dream is no different. If you feel like your dream has dulled, it's because you've forgotten something core to who you are.

In your Dream Journal, list three ways that you can better live your dream. Go ahead, do it. It will be good for you, and I believe that the answers will come easily to you.

Sometimes, when we experienced dreamers feel like our dream is missing something, it's because we are being called to leave our old mission and embark on a new one. More frequently, it's because we aren't actually living our dream – just living *with* our dream.

So get back into the arena. Help the people that you're here to help. Create what you're uniquely able to create. Unleash your passion. Choose to engage. Choose to remember. Choose to be you. Chose to *live* your dream. Because when you live your dream, miracles happen.

Sometimes you will be the recipient of these miracles. Sometimes you will be the facilitator of them. Sometimes miracles will happen that you'll never even notice, let alone begin to understand! As you fully live your dream, I promise that you WILL experience miracles. If you haven't already, I have no doubt that they are in your future.

It's a good thing, too. Your dream is big, much bigger than you now are, and you need miracles. Otherwise, you would never get off the ground! Believe me, your Big Dream needs to fly.

And it will.

Because the greatest miracle of all, is you.

It's a miracle that you're alive. It's a miracle that you're here, reading this book. It's a miracle that you have discovered your unique and priceless mission. It's a miracle that you have an opportunity before you to bless the lives of others through the perfect expression of who you are.

You are a miracle, so choose to let your light shine as brightly as the sun.

You have a dream.

Cherish it. Honor it. Live it.

The 7 Steps to Discovering Your Dream:

1. CHOOSE TO SEEK YOUR DREAM

If you want to find your dream, you need to deliberately search for it. Make the intentional choice to become a dreamer. Naysayers will call this process risky, but the greatest risk is never living at your highest potential. Decide that the answer to what YOU want to do with your life will be found by discovering your dream.

2. KNOW WHAT YOU'RE LOOKING FOR

The more clearly you can define what you want, the more direct your path to obtaining it will be. Study the principles and formulas that characterize dreams. Write out your life purpose. Reflect on your passions, aptitudes, and the needs of the world. Take the time to decide how you'll know YOUR dream when you find it.

3. FREE THE HERO WITHIN

You can't find your dream until you have taken responsibility for your life. It takes a hero to live a dream. Choose to learn of, and believe in, your divine worth and potential. Stop holding yourself back. Instead, give yourself permission to be great.

4. PAY THE PRICE FOR YOUR DREAM

Discovering your dream is as much a journey as achieving it. Sometimes, all you can see is one small step ahead. Get clear about what that next step is, and take it. It will move you in the direction of further clarity. The best way to ensure that you don't figure out what your dream is, is to sit around and wait for it to show up.

5. SUBMIT YOUR DREAM TO SOMETHING GREATER

Because a Big Dream is greater than you, it must ultimately come from a greater source. After you have paid the price for your dream, you must be willing to give it all up in exchange for something better. Trust the greatest source of light and wisdom you can find. When the time is right, your trust will be answered with a glorious mission for you to fulfil.

6. TAKE YOUR LEAP

Your dream will become real the moment you take an audacious leap of faith. Your leap of faith will ensure the survival of your dream and propel you forward with the momentum of results. Commit to your dream. Sacrifice for your dream. Take the big risk. Doing so will enable you to serve others in a greater way than ever before.

7. LOOK FOR THE MIRACLES

The presence of miracles indicate that you are living your dream. Look for them. If you can't find any, you have something to change. If miracles are surrounding you, you're on the right path. Keep going! The more you live your dream, the more miracles you will see.

Thank you for reading!

If this book has changed or greatly impacted you, consider purchasing a copy for a friend, relative, or student who is looking for their dream.

Lionheart Mentoring is always in search of leaders, champions, and heroes who are determined to live a life that exceeds all common expectations. We invite you to reach out to us personally, attend one of our events, or bring one of the Lionheart Mentors out to speak at your school, conference, or seminar.

To do so, visit:

LionheartMentoring.com

Alternatively, search for @LionheartMentoring on social media, or email us at LionheartMentoring@gmail.com.

You are a dreamer; choose to live like one.

Made in the USA
San Bernardino, CA
14 October 2017